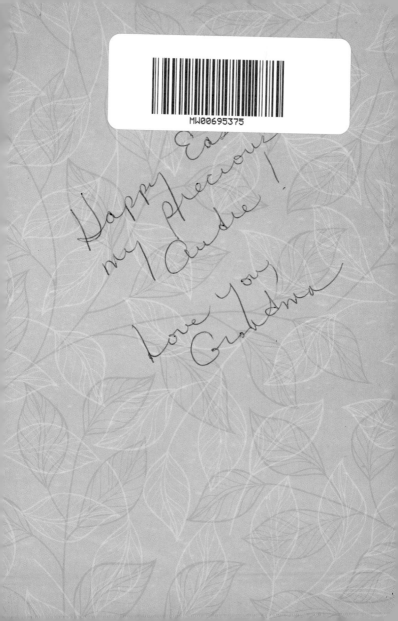

Happy Ea[ster]
my precious
Audie!

Love You
Grandma

365
Days of Prayer
for
Life

BroadStreet
PUBLISHING

BroadStreet Publishing Group LLC
Savage, Minnesota, USA
Broadstreetpublishing.com

365 Days of Prayer for *Life*
© 2020 BroadStreet Publishing

978-1-4245-6013-4
978-1-4245-6014-1 (ebook)

Composed by Sara Perry.

Design by Chris Garborg | garborgdesign.com
Compiled and edited by Michelle Winger | literallyprecise.com

Printed in China.

20 21 22 23 24 25 7 6 5 4 3 2 1

Don't worry about anything;

instead, pray about everything.

Tell God what you need,

and thank him for all he has done.

PHILIPPIANS 4:6 NLT

Introduction

Whether you have made prayer a habit for many years or this is your first prayer devotional, inspiration is waiting for you in the daily prayers written here. Ultimately, prayer is a conversation with God. You don't need to use fancy words or recite long passages of Scripture. Just talk to God. Open your heart. He adores you, and he's listening to every word you say.

Some days your prayers may be filled with gratitude, some days with repentance, and some with need. Just lay your heart and your prayers at the Father's feet and wait for his powerful response.

May God bless you as you connect daily with him.

As you develop a habit of prayer, think about this:

PRAISE

Begin by telling God how wonderful he is. Focus on which of his many attributes you are grateful for.

REPENTANCE

Before you present your needs to God, pause. Take a moment to examine your heart. If God reveals any unconfessed sin, bring it before him and ask for forgiveness.

ASK

What do you need from your Father in heaven today? Ask him boldly; he is waiting to grant you the desires of your heart.

YIELD.

Ask as if it will be done and yield to his will. Acknowledge he may know something you don't or have something even better in mind for you. Trust and accept whatever answer you receive.

January

The earnest prayer of
a righteous person has
great power and produces
wonderful results.

JAMES 5:16 NLT

Perfect Plan

Many are the plans in a person's heart,
but it is the Lord's purpose that prevails.

PROVERBS 19:21 NIV

Father, I am so grateful for the reminder that your mercies
are new every morning. I feel that in a real way on this
New Year's Day. God, you know the plans that have been
forming in my heart for the days, weeks, and months
ahead. Some are small and some are big, but whether
these plans work out or not, help me to always yield
my heart to your purpose. Help me to see the ways that
you are working when things are working out well and
especially when my plans fall apart.

Whatever this year brings, I begin it with the intention of
leaning into you, no matter what. Today, I join my dreams
to yours and invite you into the nitty-gritty of the present
moment. May my heart stay joined with yours through
both the mundane and the changes that life brings. You are
the Lord of my life.

What would you like to see change this year?

Choosing Well

Trust in the LORD with all your heart,
And lean not on your own understanding;
In all your ways acknowledge Him,
And He shall direct your paths.

PROVERBS 3:5-6 NKJV

Lord, I come to you today with an open heart and mind, trusting you to lead me. My go-to move is to try to work things out in my own understanding, but that often leads to worry and exhaustion. I know that your ways are higher than my ways and that you see the bigger picture. Today, I'm letting go of my need to control how things turn out. I lean into your love and trust that you know what you're doing much better than I do. Help me to remember that you are a good father, always directing me with gentleness and wisdom.

When I start to feel anxious about the future, I will take a deep breath and remember that you are the one who guides me. I am not alone, and I can trust you to be with me every step of the journey. Thank you, God.

Are you ready to trust God completely with your life?

Work that Matters

Whatever you do, work heartily,
as for the Lord and not for men.

COLOSSIANS 3:23 ESV

Good Father, you are the author and sustainer of my faith. Help me to keep you at the forefront of my mind when I could so easily get frustrated by tasks that go unseen, are overlooked, or are taken for granted by those around me. When I feel the temptation to throw up my hands and say, "What's the use? What is this for?" help me to remember that even if no one else sees the value of what I'm doing, you see it.

I so often get caught up in the never-ending to-do list on the hamster wheel of life. When it comes to work, it all matters to you, not because that's where I find my worth, but because you see it all and give it value. Nothing is overlooked by you. May I keep a humble heart that is connected to your love in every moment. Let every act I do be as a fragrant offering of worship to you.

What is your reason for doing all your tasks?

Positive Influence

"Let your light shine before men in such a way
that they may see your good works,
and glorify your Father who is in heaven."

MATTHEW 5:16 NASB

Wonderful God, you are brighter than the sun; your ways shine brilliantly in a dark world. Lord, I have joined my life to yours. May my life reflect your glory! I will not hoard the goodness you've placed in my life, living as if my interests are the only ones that matter. If I keep my light hidden, what's the point?

Lord, I know that you have given me everything I need to live a life like yours. As I love others with mercy, may they realize how incredibly merciful you are. As I live with a heart of compassion toward all, may others catch on to how compassionate you are. When I treat others with kindness, no matter their station or attitude, may it be a reflection of your own inclusive kindness. Let all I do line up with your character. When it doesn't, let me be quick to repent and seek forgiveness and reconciliation, revealing your magnanimous heart that is swift to forgive. Be glorified in my life.

How do your actions reflect the heart of the Father?

Send Friends

If either of them falls down,
one can help the other up.
But pity anyone who falls
and has no one to help them up.

ECCLESIASTES 4:10 NIV

Compassionate One, you are an ever-present help in time of trouble. Whenever I stumble, there you are with your strong arms to catch and hold me. I have known your faithful presence as my constant support in every season. No one matches your grace, but let your people do their best. I'm so grateful for a community of friends who have stuck with me through thick and thin. They have been there through my darkest days and are a constant source of encouragement, solidarity, and aid. I see you in them!

For those going it alone with you, I pray that you send friends so they would know the beauty of life shared with others who are seeking to live for you. Let your mercy flow through us, to one another and out into the world. A shared load is lighter. May I walk intentionally sharing my own burden as well as helping others with theirs. Thank you that we are strengthened in family and community. Let me not be isolated from your people.

Who are your true friends?

Brought Low

When holy lovers of God cry out
to him with all their hearts,
the Lord will hear them and come to rescue them
from all their troubles.

PSALM 34:17 TPT

Yahweh, you are the one in whom I find all my longings fulfilled. There is not one good thing that could satisfy me the way that you do. Though other things may gratify me for a time, your love is consistent all the days of my life, never losing its luster. I will not hold back my heart from you today; I need you more than I can express. Come into the places of my life laid out before you. I need your restoration power in my relationships. I'm desperate for your peace to bring calm to the chaotic situations that threaten my emotional stability. Bring your wisdom into situations that are confusing, and the ones that have no easy answers. I need your love to drive out the anxieties that build in the pressure cooker of my nervous system.

God, you are everything I need. Don't turn your back when I cry out to you. I know you won't. You don't grow weary of kindly reassuring your children when they start to squirm at the unfamiliar. You are my help and my hope!

What help do you need from the Lord today?

Abide

"Abide in me, and I in you.
As the branch cannot bear fruit by itself,
unless it abides in the vine,
neither can you, unless you abide in me."

JOHN 15:4 ESV

Faithful Companion, I am so grateful that I am not meant to do life in my own strength. I can only give you a limited offering of skills, time, and resources. Yet you say that fruit is born out of abiding, of being connected. I remember today, that whatever I do, if I am connected to and rooted in you, fruit will come in time. It is so easy to get caught up in the frenzy of life and forget that you are the source of all life.

Today, I center my mind around the reality of your goodness and I remember that being connected to you is enough to produce fruitfulness. I don't need to conjure it up and work to the bone to make fruit appear. God, would you produce fruit that lasts in my life? Help me to see with fresh eyes today what leaning into you looks like.

What can you let go of today that keeps you from resting in the knowledge that you are abiding in God and he in you?

Fully Committed

"Devote yourselves completely to the Lᴏʀᴅ our God, walking in his statutes and keeping his commandments, as at this day."

1 KINGS 8:61 NRSV

Son of God, I am so grateful that I have in you the perfect example of what it looks like to be devoted fully to the Father. When it feels impossible to give you everything, I am reminded that walking with you is an epic journey, not a short stroll. Thank you that you are incredibly patient with me, even in my wandering and failures. Devotion does not require perfection, only a heart and life yielded to your love. In keeping with that, I will not live under the weight of shame that declares if it isn't perfect, it isn't worth anything.

Thank you, God, that as I keep coming back to you, I am reminded that your grace and mercy are what keep me connected to your loving heart. That is the only way I can remain in you, pouring out my love and walking in your ways. Here I am again, Lord, committed to you, because, oh Faithful One, you are committed to me.

What has been holding you back from being fully devoted to the Lord?

Deliver Me

"Lead us not into temptation,
but deliver us from the evil one."

MATTHEW 6:13 NIV

Constant One, as long as I live, I will find myself faced with temptations to turn away from you. I am grateful that you are not aloof, unconcerned and hands-off with your people. You constantly draw me back to you with loving-kindness.

As I face this day, help me to resist the temptations that are bound to come my way and keep my heart set on you. Deliver me, oh God, from things that seem beneficial but are actually parasitic—slowly sucking the life right out of me. Let your loyal love keep me rooted in the wisdom that walking with you brings. May I taste your goodness, and may that goodness sustain my heart, strengthening me to choose you time and time again. When I face temptation and resist, I find that the fruit of self-control and peace are worth it every time. You always know better, and I will lean into your wisdom.

*Do you trust that God gives the strength
you need to resist temptation?*

Accountable

Each one must answer for himself and give a personal account of his own life before God.

ROMANS 14:12 TPT

God who sees all, you alone know the true state of my life and heart. Everything I do is laid plainly before you, and all that I am is mine to own. Thank you that your requirement is not perfection; rather, it is a submitted life. I ask that you keep my heart sensitive, and I give you permission, Holy Spirit, to hold me accountable in the here and now. May I be quick to repent when you show me the error of my ways. With your Spirit living in me, I can trust you to convict me when I am wrong.

You are kind in correction, leading me to repentance. Let me be a person who humbly admits my faults and submits to the process of being made whole. You, as always, are better than I've known. I align my life with your law of love today and every day.

What keeps you accountable in your daily life?

So Much Grace

From his fullness we have all received,
grace upon grace.

JOHN 1:16 NRSV

Lord, in the craze of life and responsibilities, it is so easy for me to forget the grace that I undeservedly live under. Gracious God, you give out of the fullness of your being. You are not lacking in love or running low on mercy. You are like a rushing river of life, ever-flowing, never receding.

Today I am reminded that where I have seen lack, you see an opportunity—a place that is ready to receive kindness out of the abundance of your character and kingdom. It makes no difference to you if my need is spiritual, physical, or emotional, you have more than enough to fill every dry and arid place and make it new. You make it into a place of growth and beauty. I invite you into these hard places and spaces in my life. Don't hold back, God, you have access to all of it!

What areas of your life need God's grace to flood them?

Loneliness

Even if my father and mother abandon me,
the LORD will hold me close.

PSALM 27:10 NLT

Constant Companion, even when I feel utterly alone in this life, I know that you are with me. You don't stay with me simply out of obligation. No, you lovingly hold me together when I feel like my world is falling apart. You take what looks broken beyond repair and make it completely new—no one would know that it was ever broken. When it seems like no one understands me or is interested in who I am, you are the one who sticks closer than a brother.

Your loyal love wakes me up from the slumber of disappointment and apathy. I want to experience the confidence of your presence today, Lord. Flood my day with reminders of your nearness; even now, I can't help but thank you for your kindness. As you have been with me until now, so you will always be. I am so grateful.

How have you seen the Lord's presence in your life?

Refresh and Restore

It is in vain that you rise up early
and go late to rest,
eating the bread of anxious toil;
for he gives to his beloved sleep.

PSALM 127:2 ESV

Restorer, you are the source of peace that I long for. It is like second-nature to get caught up in endless working, but your way is so much better. Creator, when you formed this world and breathed life into flesh and bone, you took time to revel in your work. You patterned us for rest, and I must admit that I have not been taking that seriously. Thank you that we are not slaves, endlessly toiling for a cruel master.

You are a good father, gently instructing and guiding us. I will not eat of the bread of anxiety today that says there is so much more to do; I will partner with you, and when my work is done, I will rest and play and be restored. Help me to take rest seriously, especially living in a society that is always demanding more than can ever be done.

*What can you do today to establish rest
as a ritual and not a luxury?*

A Heart that Would

I plead with you to give your bodies to God because of all he has done for you. Let them be a living and holy sacrifice—the kind he will find acceptable. This is truly the way to worship him.

ROMANS 12:1 NLT

Holy God, I offer you all I am today. I cannot hold back from you, knowing the extent of your loving goodness poured over my life. May my life be an offering to you, poured out in love. As I walk through my day, I will choose to walk in the way of compassion. I will choose kindness over selfish gain. I will choose trust instead of control. I will choose peace over pushing my own agenda.

Lord, I trust that as I live intentionally with my heart offered to you, you will be glorified. May the fragrance of my life of worship be pleasing to you. You are worthy of everything in my life. When I start to get caught up in the to-dos, remind me that it is the inner world from which everything flows. May the fingerprints of your goodness mark my heart and my life as I journey with you.

Is there any part of your heart that you're holding back from God?

Accepting Others

As it is in your heart, let it be in mine.
Christ accepted you, so you should accept each other,
which will bring glory to God.

ROMANS 15:7 NCV

God, I'm so grateful that you are not exclusive with your love. I, on the other hand, have limits to the love that I naturally give to others. But how can I refuse to accept others when you have welcomed me with open arms? I want to be like you, Jesus, welcoming my brothers and sisters without condition. According to your Word, there isn't a difference between slave or free, male or female, Jew or Greek—they are all the same in you.

God you don't set a precedent of favoritism, so why should I? As you have loved, so let me love. Your beautiful example of compassion and acceptance broke the mold of expectation, cultural norms, and religious rites. Your kingdom is not about my comfort, and I will not let my biases keep me from seeing others as you do. Fill me with your love that I may see others whom the world overlooks.

*Is there someone in your life that you
have been struggling to accept?*

Run to Win

Do you not know that in a race all the runners run,
but only one gets the prize?
Run in such a way as to get the prize.

1 CORINTHIANS 9:24 NIV

God of my days, I commit all I am to you; my life is yours. As I run this race of life, I am so grateful for your constant presence that fills me with everything I need right when I need it. I will not give up hope when the weather changes; I won't lose heart when obstacles come. Will you coach me to know when to rest and when to run; when I should go hard with everything I have and when to take it slow and steady? I know that when I ask you for help, you won't ignore me.

You are the best teacher I could ever have; I depend on you. Keep me in my lane when I would rather jump into someone else's. Give me all the wisdom and discernment I need to keep my eyes fixed on the end goal not on the challenge of the present terrain. I trust you, God. All this is for you.

*Are you caught up in the cares of the present,
or are you living with the end in view?*

Forgiven

> "Whenever you stand praying, forgive, if you have anything against anyone; so that your Father in heaven may also forgive you your trespasses."
>
> MARK 11:25 NRSV

Merciful God, you are full of forgiveness for those who humble themselves before you. You know that I want to live in the light of your truth. I repent of my selfish ways. I don't want my own way just so I can live pleasing myself. It's not worth it! Give me the grace I need to extend forgiveness to those who hurt me. I don't want to hold grudges, God, knowing that they are like rust, eating away at my own soul. I have been forgiven of so much; I live in the freedom that your compassion extends.

Lord, when I am struggling to forgive those who have wronged me, would you give me the grace to choose it—and choose it again—until my heart is not triggered in anger or sadness by the thought of them. I lay down every complaint I've been holding onto. The weight is not worth it.

Who can you forgive today?

Gifts in Disguise

Give thanks in all circumstances;
for this is the will of God in Christ Jesus for you.

1 THESSALONIANS 5:18 ESV

Good God, today I come to you with an open heart and intentions set on you. Where I would normally react in negativity to unexpected challenges in my day, help me to turn it into gratefulness. I know that you can use anything to better me, and I want to be more like you. When testing comes, may I learn to creatively turn it into an opportunity to find something to be thankful for. There is no circumstance that does not have potential to be turned into a place of praise.

May I become a master praise-spinner, seeing the openings for your love to shine through. As I practice the habit of gratitude, I know that it will come easier; I will more quickly see the areas that whisper your mercy. However big or small, every situation can be turned on its head in my thought-life by finding a path of appreciation. Jesus, may you be glorified in my mind.

Can you practice gratitude in the challenges in your life?

Inspire Me

God created great sea creatures and every living thing
that scurries and swarms in the water, and every sort of
bird—each producing offspring of the same kind.
And God saw that it was good.

GENESIS 1:21 NLT

Creator, you are the most innovative being that exists.
Since I was made in your image, I realize that makes me
creative. You made me with a unique creativity that doesn't
have to look like anyone else's. Inspire me today to see the
goodness around me. When I am lacking in imagination,
I will look to your creation to see the great diversity on
display. There is no shortage of ideas in you, no lack of
new approaches. God, in you I find the resources that the
world longs for free of charge. There isn't an angle that
you haven't looked at. When I am stumped, I look to you.
Whether or not I feel like I need a fresh perspective, you
have a new one to share whenever I ask.

Today, Lord, I recognize that I do need a new view—an
aspect of creation I've never seen before. I want to
constantly learn and grow in you. Open my eyes to your
wonders expressed in magnificent ways!

Where do you find inspiration?

No Compromise

"If you love me, obey my commandments."

JOHN 14:15 NLT

Consistent One, you do not change your requirements of us from day-to-day. You are consistent in your expectations. It is so easy to think about a list of directives as a way to control others. However, you, in your infinite wisdom, know what is for our benefit and for your glory. You don't require that we live to the letter of the old law; in Jesus, it's found its fulfillment! But your greater command is that everything we do be done in love, showing mercy to those who persecute us, welcoming in the stranger, and practicing a life of compassion toward those in need, not forgetting that we were once them.

Lord, in all I do, may I love you with all my heart, mind, soul and strength, holding nothing back from you. Love is not simply a feeling; it is proven in love, in action. Your affection is unfailing; I bind myself to your loyal love. May the strength of it keep me going and living according to your Word.

Have you grown lax in following Jesus' instructions for life?

Weary

Those who wait for the Lord shall renew their strength,
they shall mount up with wings like eagles,
they shall run and not be weary,
they shall walk and not faint.

ISAIAH 40:31 NRSV

Almighty God, you have all the strength I need. You see me and how tired I am. You see how weary I am in showing up in the same capacity to the same-old over and over again. I am worn-out and don't feel like I have anything to give. But you renew those who wait on you. So, here and now, I'm waiting. I quiet the chaos of my mind in your presence, breathing deeply. Bring your peace, Lord. My body needs renewal; I'm sore and I don't have the strength to do what I could yesterday. In my weakness, I come to you. I can't pretend to have it all together right now because I certainly don't! I know that's not what you're looking for anyhow.

God, your grace gives me the strength I need to keep going. I will trust in your unfailing love that fills my tank when it is running low. Renew me. I have no hope without you.

When you are weary, where do you turn for strength?

Season of Grief

Since we believe that Jesus died and rose again, even so, through Jesus, God will bring with him those who have fallen asleep.

1 THESSALONIANS 4:14 ESV

God of all comfort, I am so grateful that you meet me in the depths of my sadness. When grief breaks my heart to pieces, you are there holding it together. You don't ask that I would get over heartbreak; you meet me in the middle of it. I am thankful for the hope of seeing my loved ones again, knowing that Jesus broke the chains of death. However, in this temporal place of suffering, you do not rub my nose in the hope to come; you let me know the depth of feeling. I know that there is healing in grief, and I will not resist it. When it feels overwhelming, though, and like I'm doing a free-fall into a deep, dark cavern with no floor, I need you to shore up the walls of my heart and create a vessel for the sadness. There is a mysterious beauty in grief, and I will embrace it, even as I hate the loss that it indicates.

God, only you can truly know the depth of our losses, and you are with us in them. Thank you for your presence at every point.

When grief sweeps into your life, how do you deal with it?

Loving Well

*"A new commandment I give to you,
that you love one another, even as I have loved you,
that you also love one another."*

JOHN 13:34 NASB

Gracious God, your love is endlessly dependable; it doesn't shift with the winds of the changing seasons. Your constant affection is the best thing I've ever known. I can't rightly compare it to anything else. It is better than the best love. When I consider how you require your children to love each other in the same way you do, I am speechless. Your love laid itself down over and over again, faithfully choosing the benefit of others over your own desires and whims.

Lord, I realize how selfish I am when you put it into flesh and blood terms like that. Even so, help me, God. I want to be like you which means I want to love like you. I am grateful that you don't require perfection just a willing and humble heart. Your love covers a multitude of sins, so as I practice loving others, a part of that process is humility, forgiveness, and quick repentance. Keep me focused on your incredible kindness when I want to give up and walk away—I know your way is better!

*How can you choose love that prefers others
over its own interests?*

Casting Burdens

Cast your burden on the LORD,
And He shall sustain you;
He shall never permit the righteous to be moved.

PSALM 55:22 NKJV

God of my heart, you are my sustainer and helper. You are the strong rock on which I stand. My feet are planted on you, and I will not be shaken. I cannot pretend that I am full of vitality right now. I have been carrying burdens, weighed down by the bulk of them. I can't handle the weight of them anymore, Lord; I've tried to carry them for as long as I could. I hear your invitation to give you my problems because I was never meant to carry them on my own. Why do I constantly forget that? I seem to pick up new ones along the way, just as I have handed off others.

Lord, my sustainer, you are the one I cling to in the storms of this life. When I lift my eyes, I see that you have been holding onto me the entire time. As a child goes to their parents with problems, I will come to you. May I be quicker to hand them over as I grow closer to you. Thank you for your faithful love.

What are you weighed down by?
Can you give your burdens to the Lord today?

Mercy upon Mercy

"They are blessed who show mercy to others,
for God will show mercy to them."

MATTHEW 5:7 NCV

Merciful God, you give away your lovingkindness to all without worrying that you'll run low. You delight in showing mercy; I want to be more like you. Your love flows from you like a neverending river whose source is deep and pure. I am confident that as I soak in your presence, I will be filled up to pour out. When I have no resources, what am I to offer?

With you, God, I have access to all the grace I could ever need to show forgiveness, kindness, and compassion to everyone who hurts or offends me. I won't hold grudges, for what good would that do? Your law of love is better than the law that requires retribution. I will rejoice in your better way that offers life to all who would receive it. I can't help but be filled with joy as I align myself with your kingdom, knowing that even in my hardest moments and days, you are worth laying my rights down for.

Have you been holding onto a grudge?
How can you extend mercy instead?

Quick to Listen

Take note of this: Everyone should be quick to listen,
slow to speak and slow to become angry.

JAMES 1:19 NIV

Holy One, you are the example that I hold my life up to.
When I look at the world around me, it's easy to spot those
who are doing better than I am in temperance, and others
who it's clear need a lot of grace and healing to get there.
If I were to measure myself by others, the standard would
change based on who I was looking at. I won't fall into that
trap! When I look at you and your ways, I find the perfect
measure. What a glorious mystery that I am not required
to match your perfection on my own, but in you, I have
become perfected. It's almost too much to comprehend!

Lord, when others are quick to speak their minds, you are
patient in listening, truly hearing us out. May I be the same
way, patient in listening and slow to anger. Oh, Lord, that
my heart would respond, as yours does, in understanding,
drenched in compassion.

Are you quicker to speak or to listen?

Forever Gifts

When God chooses someone and graciously imparts gifts to him, they are never rescinded.

ROMANS 11:29 TPT

Faithful One, you are the giver of all good gifts. As a good father, you give out of the generosity of your heart and the bounty of your resources. You always have more than enough. Lord, your gifts, when imparted, are never taken away. Even the best things I've ever received pale in comparison to what I've received from you. There's so much, where do I even begin? Your boundless mercy and faithful love, your all-encompassing presence that is always with me—these are just a few of the myriad gifts every child of yours has been given. There are more that are specific to my life, and I am so thankful for each one.

May I not take you, or this open, loving relationship for granted, Lord. Let your compassion cover my heart and move me to share your incredible character with those around me, that we would all benefit together. Keep my heart soft as I recount all the ways you show up in your unfailing love.

What are some of the gifts that God has given you?

While I Wait

Be strong, and let your heart take courage,
all you who wait for the LORD!

PSALM 31:24 ESV

My God, you are not far away. I believe that even if I have to say it over and over again. You are not far away! Here where my feet are planted and my shoulders are carrying the weight of the situations I'm in, I cry out for your help again. I need you, God, oh, how I need you. In the waiting, whether it's for breakthrough, a promise to take shape, healing, or rescue, I will not forget to look back on my history with you.

I see your faithfulness running like a thread through my life; you have brought me through everything I have ever faced, and you won't stop now. My heart finds courage when you speak; I can feel your strength filling me up as my faith is rising. I'll remember what you've done in the past so I can take hope for the future. You won't let me down.

What encourages you in times of waiting?

Every Good Thing

Every good thing given and every perfect gift is from
above, coming down from the Father of lights,
with whom there is no variation or shifting shadow.

JAMES 1:17 NASB

Good Father, you are full of kindness toward your children.
There are no hidden motives in you. You don't change your
mind after you decide something. You don't give a gift and
then take it back, threatening your children so they will
stay in line. That's not how you work. You are better than
the best parent. Your motives are not selfish. They are pure
love poured out. You know better than any of us, leading
us in the kindness of your heart. Your gifts are a reflection
of your character; they don't go against it. I will not be
confused what is from you and what is not because the
fruit of it makes it abundantly clear.

I am so thankful for your generous heart that continually
pours out to those who love you. May I always stay in this
open space of receiving, leaving the doors of my heart
open to you and your influence. There is no better love in
all the earth!

What good gifts do you see in your life?

Speak of Love

If you confess with your mouth the Lord Jesus and believe in your heart that God has raised Him from the dead, you will be saved. For with the heart one believes unto righteousness, and with the mouth confession is made unto salvation.

ROMANS 10: 9–10 NKJV

Jesus, you are the Lord over all. Your great love poured out unto death, and in resurrection power, you were raised back to life. You defeated the grave, rendering death powerless. I believe that you are the only one who saves. Yours is the kingdom and the glory forever. As I align myself to you, Lord, fill me with everything I need for a life of faith. You have all the peace, all the love, all the courage, all the joy— everything I could ever think to ask for and more.

God, in your great power, I invite you to fill my life with your mercy. May it leak out of my life all over those I come in contact with throughout my day. Let your grace flow like a river to touch those I live and work with. My heart is submitted to yours. Have your way in me, King of kings!

How do you see the love of Jesus working in your life?

Gentleness

Remind the people to be subject to rulers and authorities, to be obedient, to be ready to do whatever is good, to slander no one, to be peaceable and considerate, and always to be gentle toward everyone.

TITUS 3:1-2 NIV

God of kindness, you exhibit the strength of compassion to all who look to your example. The characteristics of your kingdom seem so upside-down next to the world's ways. Instead of using the strength of weapons to intimidate, you call us to the pathway of peace. Instead of demanding perfection from others, we consider each other in humanity, treating each other with kindness and respect. We peaceably follow the laws of the land as put together by the authorities. We don't slander or insult others if they have a different perspective than we do. Clothed in gentleness, we are lights that cannot be hidden.

Lord, looking at the way you call us to live, I realize that I am out of sync in a few areas. Forgive me for the areas where I have chosen to dig my heels into my own opinion, rather than extend love, compassion, and the benefit of the doubt to others. I want to walk in your way.

Does your life reflect the radical way of love?

February

Look to the LORD
and his strength;
seek his face always.

1 CHRONICLES 16:11 NIV

First Stone

When they persisted in asking Him, He straightened up,
and said to them, "He who is without sin among you,
let him be the first to throw a stone at her."

JOHN 8:7 NASB

Merciful Father, you are so patient. I, on the other hand,
struggle to forgive those who have hurt me. When I look
at the example that Jesus set and the way he not only
forgave those who tortured and hurt him, but also called
others to compassion, I can't help but question my reactive
heart. Baptize my heart with your love, so patience,
compassion, and grace would be an overflow of your life
inside me. You are the source of every resource I need
for every situation and person I face. There is no one that
can exhaust the limits of your great affection. I want to be
found there, swimming in the depths of it.

I cannot give away what I don't have myself, Lord, so fill
me again today. I am humbled by your great patience and
challenged by your advocacy of the poor, hurting, and
voiceless. I join myself to you today, Jesus; I ask for vision
to see those around me with eyes of compassion, backed
up with a heart called to action.

What stones have you been ready to hurl at others
that you can lay down today?

All I Need

My God will supply every need of yours according
to his riches in glory in Christ Jesus.

PHILIPPIANS 4:19 ESV

God over all, you freely provide for every need with the
abundance of your kingdom. There is no area of lack that
you overlook or ignore. Give me a shift in perspective
where I have not been able to recognize your provision, and
an open heart to receive what you willingly give. I am so
grateful that your faithfulness is not dependent on my own
faith. Even so, Lord, I want to be one who believes that you
are who you say you are. You are better than I've known.

When I look back over my life, I see your faithful presence
marking my story. I know that you never change, and you will
continue to faithfully lead, guide and provide all I'll ever need
in your love. Until I see clearly, and all mysteries are made
known, let me hold fast to the one who holds fast to me.

How have you seen God provide in your life?

Simple Pleasures

I've learned from my experience
that God protects the childlike and humble ones.
For I was broken and brought low,
but he answered me and came to my rescue!

PSALM 116:6 TPT

Holy One, I have been carrying around my burdens, trying to do it all on my own. When did I start believing that stress and worry are holy endeavors? Your Word says that you protect the childlike and humble ones. I don't know many children who worry about whether they are doing enough; they trust that their parents will take care of the big stuff and they just get to be themselves.

Today, Lord, I remember what it was like to not expect myself to be the one to make things happen in my life. I trust that even in my brokenness you consistently come to my rescue. You see what I cannot and you are more powerful to save than I could ever be. I trust you, remembering that I am your child and you are taking care of me. I trust you with my life. What joy to be found in relationship to you.

How can you practice being childlike today?

Power Supply

He gives power to the faint,
and strengthens the powerless.

ISAIAH 40:29 NRSV

Mighty God, where I am limited, you are limitless. I center myself in the knowledge of your love that meets me wherever I am. When I feel like I have nothing more to give, when my body is physically sick and unable to do what it once could, I will call on you for help. When my emotional capacity is running dangerously low, let me remember that you are the source in which all my needs are met. Though I reach the limits of my humanity on a regular basis, you embody the abundance of life. Instead of beating myself up for not being stronger or able to do more, I will look to you—the pursuer of my heart, the mighty one who fights for me.

Every battle I face is an opportunity to lean into your love, where all strength and power is found. I cannot do this on my own, nor do I want to. Strengthen me today with the power of your presence within and around me. I need you.

What weakness can you invite God's strength into today?

No Small Miracle

You are the God who performs miracles;
you display your power among the peoples.

PSALM 77:14 NIV

Creator God, you are the one who formed the heavens and set the stars into motion. You are the one who set the earth on its axis, who spoke and ideas became a tangible reality. You molded flesh and breathed life into dry bones. Since the beginning, you have been the life-giver, and you are the same today as you have always been. There are no small miracles to you; you still display your power to people all around the world.

Today I'm asking to have eyes to see miracles—things that only you can do. Thank you for the breath in my lungs right this very moment and for a new day that has yet to unfold. I don't want to miss you today, Lord. May my eyes see, my heart understand, and my body carry out the miracles that are all around. There is no one like you.

If you think about the impossible being done,
when was the last time you saw or heard of a miracle?

Inspired to Please

"Be careful! When you do good things, don't do them in front of people to be seen by them. If you do that, you will have no reward from your Father in heaven."

MATTHEW 6:1 NCV

Lord, in a world full of ambition, help me to remember that you are the ultimate audience. Give me a heart that rests in the fact that nothing I do out of a heart of love is overlooked by you. When I work for the good of those around me, I ask that you keep my mind coming back to the truth that whether or not it is seen or recognized by those around me, it is worth doing. Help my heart to remain humble and down to earth in its intentions that I wouldn't be looking for recognition or praise from others. Good things done without a true heart get instant satisfaction; however, the greater return of investment will not be received.

I'm playing the long-game here, fully invested in you even when the return feels small in the moment. I don't want actions without the heart behind it, and neither do you. You have my heart; let my offerings be out of the overflow of a life lived for you.

If you look at the way you live your life, both privately and publicly, do you see a difference between the attitude of your heart?

Confidence

Do not throw away your confidence,
which has a great reward.

HEBREWS 10:35 NCV

Holy One, you are my confidence. I don't trust in the strength of my own abilities or in the faithfulness of even my closest friends. There's not much in life that I am truly certain of, but may I never doubt that you are my great reward. Whatever happens in life, would you keep me tucked into your side, covered in your loyal love and great grace? Even when my confidence wavers in religious systems, and what I thought were non-negotiable beliefs are shown to simply be tradition painted as piety, may my heart stay tethered to yours. You don't deal in manipulation or fear; it's not how you operate. When I question perhaps everything else, may your love be the staying force.

I cannot despise a life lived out of true affection. Your ways, Jesus, are beautiful, and I want to follow you. The cost may be great, but the reward will be worth it—far beyond anything I can imagine with my limited creativity.

What are you most confident about?

Remain Faithful

If we are faithless, he remains faithful—
for he cannot deny himself.

2 TIMOTHY 2:13 ESV

Faithful Father, you are undeniably good in your constancy. You don't go back on your promises even when I lose all faith. How can that be? Thank you that your follow-through is not dependent on my own. I am so grateful that your Word is your honor. It is such a relief to realize that you are bigger, better, and more steady than I can imagine. When I start to wander and wonder, lead me back to you in your loving-kindness.

As the psalm says, your faithfulness stretches to the skies. It is beyond my understanding though it blows me away with your goodness at every new level of revelation. As you are faithful, may I reflect you in this way, becoming more and more like you. Thank you for a new day to experience your unwavering pursuit; you are so worthy of my praise.

How has God's faithfulness changed your life?

Everything Changes

Be diligent in these matters;
give yourself wholly to them,
so that everyone may see your progress.

1 TIMOTHY 4:15 NIV

Lord, in this life, things shift all the time. As seasons change, so do we. You are the constancy in a world full of instability. My God, as I partner with you in this life may the ways of your kingdom become my ways. Let my values be marked by yours, that I may expand into a full-grown child of the King. As I grow, may I mature; as I mature, may I humbly become a vessel of your love. Let everything I do be laced with your character—full of love, patience, kindness, joy, compassion, and peace.

As the shifting winds of change roll in, I remain tethered to you, knowing you've got me even when I can't see the way. I know you are much more invested in who I am rather than what I do for you, so I press into the ocean of your kindness as I navigate this life with you. Let me become more and more like you, loving God and faithful friend.

How do you react to change?

Light, Love, and Truth

Peter and the apostles replied,
"We must obey God rather than any human."

ACTS 5:29 NLT

Infinite One, I owe everything I am and everything I have to you. I would rather spend my days living in the law of your love than anywhere else. Today, I consecrate myself to you, asking for your wisdom to guide me into all truth. I want to be aligned with you and your ways. Lord, keep me on the narrow path that chooses love above all other things: above my own comfort, preferences, and other's expectations. Your ways are better than my own and better than what others require as well. May I stay true to you and your Word as I walk this path with you.

Today, let my choices reflect your ways rather than my own. Help me to stay fixed on you, the author and perfecter of my faith. When I begin to default to my own biases, Holy Spirit, would you remind me of the wisdom of your Word and ways. I yield my heart and my choices to you today.

What does it mean for you to obey God today?

The Mirror

If anyone is in Christ, there is a new creation: everything old has passed away; see, everything has become new!

2 CORINTHIANS 5:17 NRSV

Gracious One, I am so grateful that every day is a new beginning with you. Every moment is a brand-new opportunity to be intentional. Even more, you have said that if I am in you, I am a new creation. I have been made new, and even when I look back over my journey with you, if my "new" body is feeling like it's wearing down, you make me new again! Your love never grows stale and your grace never grows old.

You are always in the present though you are not confined to it. I take this time right now in my day to invite you into this moment. Breathe life into me again, blowing away the dust of the world and its weight. Wash me in the light of your goodness, that all the darkness of doubt and the lies that so easily entangle me would be washed away. Your Word says that "whom the Son sets free is free indeed." Let everything that has bound me fall off now in the name of Jesus, that I may walk freely with you in the land of the living.

What areas of your life need a new touch from God?

Not Good

I know what it is to be in need, and I know what it is to
have plenty. I have learned the secret of being content
in any and every situation, whether well fed or hungry,
whether living in plenty or in want.

PHILIPPIANS 4:12 NIV

God, I am so grateful that my relationship with you is not
dependent on my circumstances. You are a good father,
who does not love his kids more when they succeed and
less when they fail. Your love is the steadiest thing in the
universe. Whatever my life looks like right now—the good,
the bad, the ugly—is where you meet me. I don't need
wealth or success to be content. I also don't need to live
with barely anything to my name to live in the simplicity of
your gospel.

Lord, as I lean into your heart today, impart the fruit of
your character into my life that my satisfaction would be
found in relationship to you. When I struggle and fall, I
have as much access to your goodness as when everything
seems to be going well. Today, you know right where I
am on that spectrum. I welcome you, Holy Spirit, to bring
revelation light to my life and to the meaning of life. I know
that I will find it in you.

Does your belief about God and how he sees you change
when your circumstances shift?

Let you In

Search me, O God, and know my heart;
test me and know my anxious thoughts.

PSALM 139:23 NLT

Oh God, search out my heart and my mind, looking right into the core of every matter. You see the worries furrowed across my brow and the questions I wrestle with on a consistent basis. You don't pretend to not see what is circling in my thoughts. I don't need to hide them from you. When I don't know how to form a prayer about these things, hear my heart and answer the cries that remain under the surface. In your wisdom, give divine answers and solutions to problems that cannot be solved by my own logic. I know the mark of your move in my life; it always feels like peace and looks like something better than I could know how to ask for.

Today, let your Word breathe peace into my mind, calming and dispelling anxious thoughts. Let the swirl of worry be calmed like bodies of water after a storm. Thank you for your kind care of me in every season. I love you.

Can you give God control of your thoughts today, inviting him into that space to bring peace to worries and anxiety?

You Are Love

He who does not love does not know God,
for God is love.

1 JOHN 4:8 NKJV

God of kindness, your love knows no limits or boundaries.
It is an infinite resource; it's so much more than a feeling,
and much more than I can rightly know. Your Word
says that you are love. It is your very character. What a
wonderful mystery. There are so many expressions of this
lavish, loyal love that I can see in my life and all around
me. The weight of your affection is staggering, and yet it
is the most refreshing force on earth. It's like a cool breeze
on a hot day and refreshing water in the desert. It is the
strongest force in the universe. How could it not be if it is
who you are?

You are so good, Lord. Let my life be filled with this love
that demonstrates my identity as a child of the one true
God. Increase my capacity! I want to know how high, how
deep, how wide, how long is your love. It may be a futile
request, for who could know its lengths? Even so, Lord, I
want more.

Where do you see the thread of God's love?

One Heart

"I will give them one heart, and put a new spirit within them. And I will take the heart of stone out of their flesh and give them a heart of flesh."

EZEKIEL 11:19 NASB

God of redemption, thank you for your relentless love that pursues my heart at every point in life. You do not require my perfect obedience or submission in order to do what you set out to do. You have taken my cold, cold heart and given me a heart that beats with the warmth of your love. You took what was hard and indifferent and replaced it with a moldable, movable organ. Thank you for your fluid grace, that does not do anything the same way but is always recognizable in its character. I welcome you to move again in me, to open my eyes to this one heart you have given all your people.

Thank you for your Spirit that has brought life to me in every possible way. May I walk humbly with you, with a heart of flesh that is connected to the ultimate source of lifeblood found in you. I remember that I am part of a family with the same heart; may it be undivided.

*Can you see a difference in your heart
as you walk with the Lord?*

Every Opportunity

Don't allow yourselves to be weary or disheartened in planting good seeds, for the season of reaping the wonderful harvest you've planted is coming!

GALATIANS 6:9 TPT

Lord, you know how easily I can get discouraged by things not working out the way I hoped they would. But you, God, are relentlessly faithful in all you do. Thinking through my disappointments right now, I remember that you are a God of redemption, always faithful to come through and make things new. I will not give up planting the seeds of your kingdom life, even if I don't see growth happening right now before my eyes. I hand you the weight of the discouragement I've felt and ask for your blanket of peace to rest on me. Let faith rise as I continue; strengthen me as I hold on to hope.

Empower me to love the way you love, not being exclusive or withholding. I trust that as I persevere in hope, you will come through as you always do. Let my life be marked with your life, Jesus, that all would know the freedom and joy that you bring.

What opportunities do you have to show the character of God to others?

Illusion of Control

Give yourselves completely to God.
Stand against the devil, and the devil will run from you.

JAMES 4:7 NASB

God, you are the source of every good and perfect gift.
Your words are laced with love, peace, and joy. Even in
correction, you are kind and good. I give you all I am, Lord.
You can have it all. I invite you in, Holy Spirit, to search all
of me. Guide me in wisdom and all truth. Let my feet stay
on the path of your great love that covers everything. I
don't need to have all the answers in order to follow you.

Today and every day, I follow you. Your Word says that the
devil, our enemy, has come to steal, kill, and destroy. You
have come to give life that never ends. I would rather be
found with you in the light of life, yielding to the mystery,
than struggle in the darkness of fear with logic as my only
guide. I pray that today I will be filled with peace as I walk,
surrendered to you.

*How has fear kept you from giving yourself
completely to God?*

Anger Rising

"In your anger do not sin":
Do not let the sun go down while you are still angry.

EPHESIANS 4:26 NIV

Jesus, I'm so grateful that you walked this earth and subjected yourself to the human experience. When man and woman were created, it was done in the image of God. Our emotions are a reflection of your own, and we are made to feel deeply just as you do. Son of God, you are familiar with every aspect of temptation that we face. "In your anger do not sin" is not "anger is a sin." Jesus, you got angry in the temple when you saw what was being done against the heart and intention of the Father.

God of my heart, help me to not shut down emotion that is right to feel in the moment; also, give me wisdom to not let it escalate into rage that leads me to sin. I don't know how to do that. I need your help! I trust you to help me with my anger whatever that looks like.

How do you react when you get angry?

Measured Steps

We also pray that you will be strengthened with all his glorious power so you will have all the endurance and patience you need.

COLOSSIANS 1:11 NLT

Lord, in the dark days of winter, it is hard to want to keep pressing into growth and change. Help me to remember that life is a cycle of seasons and that not every one is fruit-bearing. When I start to feel discouraged, would you give me the endurance I need to get through?

Thank you that I am your child, not your workhorse. I will press into rest, especially when the earth around me is doing the same. I will be strengthened as I lay down my expectations of effortless bounty in a season that looks like scarcity. I lean into your love, cherishing the quiet of these days and allowing myself to do less in order to be filled more. I know you will give me all the endurance and patience I need in your power. I will stop resisting the slower pace and lean back into it, knowing when the season changes that I will be ready and it will be lovely.

How can you make space in your life for intentional rest?

Pursued by Goodness

Why would I fear the future?
For your goodness and love pursue me
all the days of my life.
Then afterward, when my life is through,
I'll return to your glorious presence
to be forever with you!

PSALM 23:6 TPT

Good Father, your continual pursuit is the joy of my life. There is nowhere I can go that your love does not reach me. There is nothing I could do that would make you turn away. Your love and goodness are like a rushing river, after the rains, and I am right in its path! When I look back over my walk with you and see the goodness that you have planted in every season, why would I choose to worry about what is to come?

Today is a fresh opportunity to see your faithful love showing up in tangible ways; give me eyes to see. May my heart overflow with love for you as I continually remind myself of your goodness that marks my life. I will not miss this opportunity to practice gratitude. Thank you, God, for your unending patience with me. I delight in you because you are consistently delighting over me. How I love you!

What was the last thing God did that gave you assurance that he is with you?

Separated from Guilt

Since we have been justified by faith,
we have peace with God through our Lord Jesus Christ.

ROMANS 5:1 ESV

Gracious God, there are no words to adequately portray the greatness of who you are. You supersede every paradigm, challenging our manmade systems with your greater law of love. It is hard to comprehend the full significance of what Jesus did on the cross, making a way for us to step into the fullness of right relationship with God without any barriers to separate us.

Thank you, God, that guilt and shame are not our portion; peace with you is. Thank you, Jesus, for your incredible sacrifice that broke the chains of sin and death. Thank you for resurrection; death could not keep you in the grave, and it won't be able to do that with your children either. Thank you for life, God, not simply breath, but vibrant life. Here I am again. Fill me with the light of your truth that I may not miss a single act of your goodness.

Is there guilt you've been feeling about your relationship with God that you can let go of today?

Far Away

In God, whose word I praise,
In God I have put my trust;
I shall not be afraid.
What can mere man do to me?

PSALM 56:4 NASB

Ever-present One, you know that I have put my trust in you. Time and time again, over and over, I have given you space in my heart and my life to do what you would. When I can't see through the storm raging around me, strengthen my heart to continue to choose you. You are Emmanuel— God with us. So, I will remember that even when my heart shakes under the weight of the unknown and anxiety threatens to steal my peace.

You are with me. Let that knowledge sink into my bones until it is a part of my very foundation. You are with me. I will continue to trust you no matter what happens. You are fully aware of all the earth's goings-on. I rest in you not needing to know it all, but leaning on the one who does. You are with me, and I will be with you.

*What fear has been holding you back
from fully trusting God?*

Restraint

"Put your sword back in its place," Jesus said to him,
"for all who draw the sword will die by the sword. Do
you think I cannot call on my Father, and he will at once
put at my disposal more than twelve legions of angels."

MATTHEW 26:52–53 NIV

Lord, when I am quick to react, even to injustices, would
you give me a heart of discernment to remain true to your
kingdom's ways? As I walk with you, meditating on your
Word, may I become more like you. Thank you, Jesus, that
you are not a bully. You never took anything by force or by
demanding attention. Everything you did was done with
respect for people's humanity and dignity even when you
challenged them.

Lord, when I feel a gut reaction happening, help me to run
into a place of peace; fill my mind with your words that
bring clarity not confusion. May I be a harbinger of your
peace that brings calm to chaos. Let me not be swept up
in the passion of the moment, but may I remain steady in
your love. And when I mess up, may I be quick to ask for
forgiveness and even quicker to forgive those around me.
Thank you for your grace that empowers and enables me
to become more like you.

Are you trying to do for God, through force,
what he could do on his own but chooses not to?

Move Me

When He saw the multitudes, He was moved
with compassion for them, because they were weary
and scattered, like sheep having no shepherd.

MATTHEW 9:36 NKJV

Jesus, I have so much to learn from you: a lifetime's worth
and then some! The levels of compassion that you moved
in when you walked this earth are astounding. I know that
I must be connected to you to know true compassion
for others, and oh, how much more compassion I need
in my life. It is so easy to shut off kindness in favor of
comfort and apathy. It is easier to live in a bubble of
disconnectedness to people's pain and poverty, remaining
distant enough to recognize it but not let it upset my
comfort. However, you didn't call your disciples into a life
of ease or comfort.

I invite you today, Lord, to upset my convenience and to fill
me with compassion for those who are lost and scattered
around me. I want to share in your heart for the weary
and broken, offering love where others just keep moving
around them. Move my heart, Lord; it is open.

*Can you make space in your day to allow for God
to move your heart in compassion where you would
normally brush past it?*

Tune Me

I want you to understand what really matters, so that
you may live pure and blameless lives until the day
of Christ's return.

PHILIPPIANS 1:10 NLT

Father of love, I don't want to live an aimless life on a
winding path to nowhere. Even if I never experience the
success I hope for, if I live a life of love poured out to and
for you, then there is purpose in it. Help me to stay on
your path, not wandering over to the wide path that leads
to destruction. I want to know you and to choose you
because you chose me and know me through and through.
It's not about obligation but of delight. Fill me with your
joy that sustains through all seasons. Not superficial
happiness that changes with circumstances, but deep joy
that has known pain, walked through darkness and come
out the other side. Where joy felt impossible in the depths
of the dark valley and pain carved out a deep hole, your
love flowed in and enlarged joy's capacity.

I see that life isn't about taking the easy road but seeing
your faithful love coming through in all of the turns and
valleys and remaining connected and open through it. May
my purity be found in living a life of continual surrender; I
am yours.

What can you surrender to God today?

Sit and Wait

Wait for the LORD;
be strong, and let your heart take courage;
wait for the LORD!

PSALM 27:14 NRSV

Lord, in a world that is continually on the go, it is not my natural reaction to pull back from the pace and wait. There is very little these days that requires waiting, and therefore patience. However, I have found the richest treasures in the waiting times in my life, and I take hope that as I am waiting on you to come through in other areas, the result will be worth waiting for. Help me to let go of control of the areas where I need not micro-manage.

Help me to wait on you, Lord; fill me with strength and courage, not giving up hope that you will do what only you can do. May I rest in your Word, knowing that your promises are always fulfilled. I will not be discouraged today. I remember your faithfulness in my life and others. I have seen you do the impossible and make the possible even sweeter than I could have imagined. You are good, and it's in your goodness I rest today.

*How have you seen God move for others
who have waited on promises?*

Releasing Kindness

"Love your enemies, and do good, and lend, expecting
nothing in return, and your reward will be great,
and you will be sons of the Most High,
for he is kind to the ungrateful and the evil."

LUKE 6:35 ESV

Father, your kindness cannot be measured. You freely give out of the goodness of your heart, and I want to be just like you. Loving those who hurt and reject me and those I love is following your example. May I be one who gives without expecting anything in return, doing good because that is who you are, and you have filled my life with goodness. May I practice giving out of the abundance that you have given me, becoming more like you in your kindness. You don't ask for what you don't model, and I'm so grateful for the incredible ways you have loved me and poured out your mercy over my life.

It is not too much to be generous, if I am a child of a generous God. I pray that I would align myself in this identity. I have been well taken care of, so taking care of others and giving to those around me is a natural reflection of the reality I live in. In my kindness, may others receive your kindness, Lord.

Who can you be intentionally kind to today?

Awe Inspired

"His mercy extends to those who fear him,
from generation to generation."

LUKE 1:50 NIV

Merciful Father, it is amazing that your love spans the generations and holds the reality of our world together. Who is like you? Your faithfulness is not limited to individuals; it expands to families, communities, and nations. I realize that I have been living under your mercy all the days of my life even when I didn't know it. Thank you for people who have gone before me and for those who will come after. Will you give me vision to partner with you, not just for my own life, but for those around me as well as those I will never meet?

Today, I want to see the bigger picture. I am always encouraged when I see you or hear about you working in other's lives. Bind your people together with one heart to know that we are living under your mercy; give us vision to run together for the benefit of those who will come after us. May I run with community hand-in-hand, giving away mercy and love like life depends on it.

*Have you talked with a fellow believer lately about what
God is doing in their lives?*

Replacing Worry

Don't be pulled in different directions or worried about
a thing. Be saturated in prayer throughout each day,
offering your faith-filled requests before God with
overflowing gratitude. Tell him every detail of your life,
then God's wonderful peace that transcends human
understanding, will make the answers known to you
through Jesus Christ.

PHILIPPIANS 4:6–7 TPT

God over all, it is such an amazing privilege that I can
pour out every detail of my life to you. I don't need to be
steeped in worry about how things are going to work out
in unknown situations: what a useless waste of energy!
When I feel my mind picking up speed and starting to
bounce in different directions, help me to take over and
turn it to prayer. When I begin to feel the vines of worry
creeping in, help me to slow down and intentionally offer
those things to you in faith.

I'm grateful for every new day to practice your presence
and make you part of what I would normally try to do on
my own. Worry only ever agitates, it never calms or offers
solutions. Thank you that you work in peace, not chaos.
I'm thankful for another day to watch you bring beauty out
of ashes.

What areas of worry can you offer to God in prayer today?

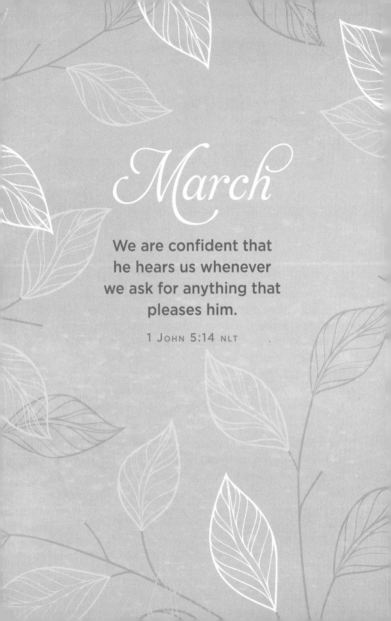

March

We are confident that
he hears us whenever
we ask for anything that
pleases him.

1 John 5:14 NLT

Change Is Good

Anyone who belongs to Christ has become a new person. The old life is gone; a new life has begun!

2 CORINTHIANS 5:17 NLT

Loving God, you are in the business of restoration. When you bring new life, you don't simply spruce up a few things or smooth out some rough edges; you do a full-scale remodel. Everything gets a major upgrade. Thank you that this is what you do in me! Where I have been stuck in old patterns, would you remind me that those are not my identity; they are not who I am in you? Breathe fresh life into me today, rejuvenating what feels dusty and old. I know that I belong to you, and that means I have your Spirit within me.

Spirit of God, I invite you to continue to change me into your likeness, making my heart more tender and open. As you increase my capacity to love like you, there is no way I could remain the same as I have been. I am connected to your life, and your life gives me everything I need. Thank you that there is nothing lacking today in order to continue to grow. You are more than enough!

Are there areas you have felt stuck in that you want to see change?

Buckling Knees

"Fear not, for I am with you;
be not dismayed, for I am your God;
I will strengthen you, I will help you,
I will uphold you with my righteous right hand."

ISAIAH 41:10 ESV

God of my strength, there are days when I feel like I can't do a thing right. When I don't have answers to big questions or the ability to solve complex problems, it is almost second-nature to feel discouraged. When life begins to spiral out of control, my heart is prone to fear. But you said that you are with me. You said don't be afraid; you are not alone. I believe you, God. I trust you. I cannot control what happens in the world around me or even in my own life sometimes, but I can let go of the need to dictate what happens and hold onto you. You always know better. Strengthen me and give me courage when I face trials of all kinds.

You know I need to be reminded; thank you for your relentless grace that prompts me to turn to you time and time again. Your patience amazes me; your constant help is my portion. I could not do this without you. Thank you for holding me up.

What fear can you release to God today?

Faith Spilling Over

"All things you ask in prayer, believing, you will receive."

MATTHEW 21:22 NASB

Lord, I come to you today with a heart longing to hear your voice. You know the constant prayers I've been offering to you; show me that you are listening, Lord, and answer me. I don't need you to reach down and turn my life around, but I do need to know you are with me in this. May my heart take courage and be filled with faith that can move mountains.

When you speak, my heart is strengthened. When you move, my courage shoots through the roof. There is nothing like knowing you. I am so grateful to be a child of the God of the universe. When I start to question whether or not you will come through, remind me who you are. You are the God of my salvation; you are the God of my yesterdays, todays, and tomorrows. You are the God who turns mourning into dancing. You are my God.

What can you ask for in faith today?

Place for Me

"There are many rooms in my Father's house;
I would not tell you this if it were not true.
I am going there to prepare a place for you."

JOHN 14:2 NCV

God over all, it is almost too much to know that the God
of the universe cares about me. When I look in your Word,
your fingerprint of love shines through nearly every page.
How amazing that you not only love us and pursue us
in this life, but you have prepared a place for us in your
kingdom. What a beautiful gift.

Lord, as I walk this life with you, when I start to get
discouraged by the world and its ways, lift my eyes.
Remind me that this life is a temporary one; there is more
to come, and it will be more wonderful than I can imagine.
Give me the endurance I need to run this race of life, not
forgetting that the finish line is the entrance to a new and
glorious reality. I won't forget that you, Jesus, have gone
ahead to prepare a place; it will be so worth the wait.

*Do you believe there is a place for you
in God's eternal kingdom?*

My Mistakes

Though he fall, he shall not be cast headlong,
for the Lord upholds his hand.

PSALM 37:24 ESV

Father of mercy, you are constantly with me, lifting me up from the depths and walking with me through the heights of life. I am so incredibly grateful that you do not expect me to be perfect; rather, it is in you that I have been perfected. Your mercy covers me in my darkest days and lifts me out of shame.

When I fall, Lord, pick me up and be the lifter of my head. May I see your eyes of love shining over me and beckoning me out of the torrent of guilt that so quickly swirls. Your love is big enough to cover every mistake and every failure. You never condemn me in my weakness; you infuse my heart with the strength of your compassion. As you cover me so willingly, forgive my every fault. May I be the same: quick to forgive and reconcile with those I am walking with through life. You are so merciful, God, and I am thankful.

Do you believe that you are defined by your mistakes or by God's great love for you?

Greater Meaning

"If a man has a hundred sheep but one of the sheep gets lost, he will leave the other ninety-nine on the hill and go to look for the lost sheep."

MATTHEW 18:12 NCV

Good Shepherd, you are the best caretaker that exists. You lead and guide us as your collective people, but you also pursue us individually. When I wander, here you come, looking for me. You won't let me fall into a trap or get caught in the enemy's lair. You are better than that. Lord, in my wandering, keep bringing me back to the fold. In the same way, when I see my brothers and sisters wandering away from your love, may I gently redirect them, reminding them of the goodness of the shepherd who is coming to meet them!

Your ways are so much better than my own; if left to my own devices, I'd be caught in a cycle of self-serving adventure-seeking. I would leave others to their own as well. Thank you for being a good leader with a watchful eye. You know the moment when I've started drifting. Keep my heart tuned to yours that I would know your goodness all the days of my life.

Do you trust that the Lord sees you when you wander and that he will rescue you?

Strength

I can do all this through him who gives me strength.

PHILIPPIANS 4:13 NIV

God of my strength, you know how much I need you. On days when it is hard to even get out of bed to face the day, fill me with strength that comes straight from you. Help me to brave the day, knowing that I have everything I need to face every obstacle that may pop up. There are no surprises to you; you aren't startled by what happens. I can rely on you to get me through every trial and circumstance; you won't let me fall.

I can face today knowing that I am yours, and you are with me. When I struggle in my weakness, you are the power that fuels my soul. Infuse me with your grace that I may courageously walk hand-in-hand with you, relying on your steady frame when my own starts to give out. I can do all things through you, Lord my God.

What do you turn to when you are tired and worn out?

Deepest Desire

"You will seek Me and find Me when you search for Me
with all your heart."

JEREMIAH 29:13 NASB

Oh Lord my hope, I know that all I'm looking for is found
in you. When I look for you, I find rest for my soul. I know
that you don't work in the same timeline that I do, but I
also believe that your ways are better and that your timing
is better than my own. Help me to trust you when I start to
lose hope. As I look for you, Lord, would you fill me with
the deep sense of satisfaction only found in knowing you?
I lay down my need for temporal things. I know you care
about my physical needs, but there is so much more to life
than having every superficial desire met.

I don't want to be like a spoiled child that does not realize
the goodness of their father because they are so caught up
in the consumerist ways of always wanting more—and that
which does not last! You are not only the source of every
good gift, you are the best one. I will let you take care of
me like a good father does, and I will press into knowing
you through time and relationship.

*Do you spend more time thinking about what you need
from God or about getting to know who he is?*

Child of the King

Your wife will be like a fruitful grapevine,
flourishing within your home.
Your children will be like vigorous young olive trees
as they sit around your table.

PSALM 128:3 NLT

Father, I am so grateful that I am a child of the King of kings. My true identity is found in relationship to you; thank you that I am not relying on my own merits. I gladly rely on you and follow your example. May I become more like you so everyone sees the resemblance as I grow in you. Good Father, I want everyone to know the goodness of your generous character. May I not take this relationship for granted. Let me remember where I came from and how you made me your own.

There is no one like you. I gladly come into your presence and lean into your embrace; there's nothing like it. When I approach you as a dearly loved child, I have confidence that you not only hear me, but you delight in my presence. I see the light in your eyes that says you're happy to see me. With the wisdom of all fathers, you give me the advice I need for every problem I'm dealing with. How could I begin to describe the joy in my heart at being your child? Thank you seems inadequate, but it's all I've got.

How do you approach God, knowing he is a good father?

My Help

I look up to the mountains and hills,
longing for God's help.
But then I realize that our true help and protection
come only from the Lord,
our Creator who made the heavens and the earth.

PSALM 121:1–2 TPT

Lord, when I feel defeated and I have nowhere to turn, I look to you. When there is no way out of the situation I'm in, I call on your name. You always provide a way through. I will not be afraid of what may come. You are the mighty conqueror. Only you can confuse the enemy and turn a situation to benefit those who love and follow you. You always know exactly what is needed. I will not tremble.

I trust in you, my God, my ever-present help in time of need. Creation bows to your intentions; the tides turn at your command. Shift the raging winds and calm the storms that surround your people. You are the only true reliable one, God of your Word. You will not turn a deaf ear when I cry to you. Here you come with more than I could think to ask for.

When was the last time you helped someone?

Drawing Me Back

May the Lord of peace himself give you peace at all times in every way. The Lord be with you all.

2 THESSALONIANS 3:16 NIV

Jehovah, in you all things find their place. You bring calm to every tumultuous situation; you release peace to the turbulent heart. Lord, today, as I live and work, may the peace of your presence be my portion. I know that you are with me, God of peace; let not my heart be troubled. Let everything I think, say, and do be saturated in the love of God that quiets chaos. You are the giver of the rest my heart needs. I know that with you, I don't need to frantically figure everything out. You give solutions to the most complicated problems.

May I be a carrier of your peace into every place my feet go today; may I be a harbinger of your love that brings unity instead of division. Let the peace of your presence not only fill me, but may it tangibly change the atmosphere around me, bringing calm to even the tensest of situations. There is no one else like you, who gives order to complete chaos. What an honor to walk with you in the path of peace.

What does the fruit of peace look like in your life?

Though I Fail

My flesh and my heart may fail,
but God is the strength of my heart
and my portion forever.

PSALM 73:26 NIV

Lord of my comings and goings, you stay consistently with me. You see my joy and my sorrow; you know my victories and my failures. Though failures make my heart heavy with discouragement, your expectations are different. You are not surprised by the way my heart and flesh get weary with my own blunders. Yet you aren't discouraged. Help me to see from your perspective that everything that turns out badly is not the end. With every breath I have, it is an opportunity to know you in a new way. I cannot exhaust your goodness; I will never reach the end of your love that makes all things new. Fill me with the light of your revelation that I may be filled with courage to start again, no matter how many new beginnings I've faced before.

All I have is this moment, and in this moment, you are the same God as you've always been. I receive your love that strengthens my heart to keep going. Thank you, Lord, that you haven't changed.

*Does God think differently of you when you fail
or when you succeed?*

Too Much

"Give, and you will receive. You will be given much. Pressed down, shaken together, and running over, it will spill into your lap. The way you give to others is the way God will give to you."

LUKE 6:38 NCV

Lord, in a world filled with people looking out for themselves, may I live for you and your kingdom. You say, "Give, and you will receive." If I am stingy with my resources, then I am not practicing a life that is open to receive from you.

Jesus, you set the ultimate example of generosity, and I want to be like you. When I am tempted to hoard my time, love, and money, help me to remember that's not what you do. I want to be like you, and I can't be like you if I'm not living a life poured out, not only in word or in the privacy of my own life, but in very practical ways. You know I am still learning this. I lean into you, practicing generosity in small moments, knowing that builds a foundation to receive from you. When I give, let me do it with a heart that doesn't expect anything in return but finds joy in others' gain. What an honor to grow in this with you.

What can you be generous with today?

Laying Down Weapons

"The LORD will fight for you,
and you shall hold your peace."

EXODUS 14:14 NKJV

Mighty God, you are my defender. I lay down my right to self-defense and demanding my side be known. I will rest in you, believing that you have got me and you will do what I could never do. Lord, when I am tempted to fight my own battles, I am reminded that you are stronger and much more capable of doing the job than I will ever be.

I won't fight for my own honor, but I will willingly hide in your shadow, letting you take the lead. I rest in you, with peace unshakeable, for you honor me even when others seek to rip me to shreds. I will not be distracted by those trying to pick a fight; no, I will keep on the track that you have put me on and let you deal with the hecklers. I will continue on the path of love, knowing I am following in your steps. I know you've got this.

Have you been fighting a battle that is wearing you down?

The Sweetest Fruit

The fruit of the Spirit is love, joy, peace, forbearance, kindness, goodness, faithfulness, gentleness and self-control. Against such things there is no law.

GALATIANS 5:22–23 NIV

Father of love, your kindness is astounding, your peace unending. Your joy is like a hidden brook, with bubbling and dancing waters flowing with life. Your goodness is found in your character; it is the very makeup of who you are. Your faithfulness is more reliable than the seasons changing. Your gentleness reveals your tender heart. Your own self-control reveals the beauty of the choices you've given us.

There is no law against these things. I could spend my whole life getting to know you in these attributes, and I would still have only scratched the surface. There are no limits to the fruit that you give. Let my life be fragrant with this fruit. In a thriving orchard, may I eat of the bounty of its fruit and also freely give it away to those around me. With a life filled with your Spirit, I cannot go wrong.

What fruit do you need more of in your life today?

Break My Heart

He was amazed to see that no one intervened to help
the oppressed. So he himself stepped in to save them
with his strong arm, and his justice sustained him.

ISAIAH 59:16 NLT

God of compassion, you are moved in lovingkindness for
those who are mistreated. How could I claim to walk with
you and not help those who cannot help themselves?
Break my heart, Lord, for what breaks yours. Let me see
the destitute around me with eyes of love, moving me
in kindness to action. Let me not be paralyzed by the
magnitude of need around me; rather, let me pray for
solutions when there are none and love those within my
grasp. I will not forget my own poverty, that I could not
stand on my own. You saved me. How much more will that
fuel me to stand with those who are fighting for freedom?

As you loved, so let me love. Jesus, you constantly
questioned and overturned oppressive ideals in favor of
unabashed, chain-breaking, rule-smashing, society-shaking
love. Your love is a fierce thing, not fluffy or cuddly; it stops
at nothing to set people free. Let my heart be rocked by
this fierce compassion!

When was the last time you felt
fierce compassion for someone?

your Motives

Am I now seeking the approval of man, or of God?
Or am I trying to please man? If I were still trying to
please man, I would not be a servant of Christ.

GALATIANS 1:10 ESV

Lord, search me and know my heart. You see every hidden motive that is there. Lord, where I tend toward pleasing the people around me over you, give me grace to choose you. I am yours; my devotion belongs to you. Help me to always prioritize you over trying to win favor with the people around me—even my leaders.

When I start to get caught up in what others think about me, I will lay down my thoughts on the altar of your love and meditate on who you say I am and who I am becoming. I will not compromise your values, or mine, by bending my obedience to satisfy someone else's preference. I will stay strong, as a child of the King, following you. May my heart remain soft, as well, that I may be molded by you and for you, my Lord. Be the leader of my life.

Who are you living to please?

Live on Purpose

The LORD has made everything for its purpose,
even the wicked for the day of trouble.

PROVERBS 16:4 ESV

Creator God, everything that was made by you was created
for a purpose. Every living thing has value. My life is not an
accident, nor was it given to me to roll through living on
chances. I believe that my life has purpose, and I want to
live it intentionally. I am so grateful that you don't leave me
to drown in the mystery. Life is a journey on paths that lead
through different terrain. I cannot avoid the arid places,
and I would not want to miss the springs along the way.

Living on purpose, with you, is to live aligned with your
kingdom and its values. With the law of love, how could I
lose? When I don't know which way to take at a fork in the
road, I will look to you and feast on the fruit of the Spirit,
knowing that you are with me no matter which way I turn.
My intentions are set on knowing you in this life and on
living for you. Be my guide, my closest friend!

Where do you find purpose in your life?

Before I Speak

To watch over mouth and tongue
is to keep out of trouble.

PROVERBS 21:23 NRSV

God, you know me inside and out. Where I struggle with temperance, especially with my mouth, I rely on you to keep me in check. Spirit of God, give me wisdom and discernment for when it is right to speak and when it is time to stay silent. In the choosing of my words, help me to remain honoring and respectful. Where there is temptation to gossip, may I instead turn the tide of conversation, or turn and walk away. There is death and there is life in the power of the tongue; your Word is clear about that.

Where I have been blasé in my approach, or just plain apathetic about what comes out of my mouth, I ask for your forgiveness. Give me resolve to be intentional about what I say and what I do not. And when I am careless, may I be quick to humbly reconcile with those I have hurt with my words. May my words be an overflow of a heart filled with your love.

Do you pause to think about what you're saying about others when they're not around?

What Is True

It is the greatest joy of my life to hear that my children are consistently living their lives in the ways of truth!

3 JOHN 1:4 TPT

Life Giver, you are the source of every good thing. When I come to you, looking for my daily portion that will give me what I need to face the day, I find even more than I asked for. Your love floods my heart and mind, lighting up my insides with revelation-knowledge. Your living Word is at work in my life; I see the fruit of truth in the ways you have transformed my thoughts. Your noble truth, which is pure, peace-loving, kind, and full of patience for parts that haven't caught up, is alive in my heart.

Thank you, Lord, that as I live with and for you, you are filling every part of my life with the joy that knowing you brings. Today, Lord, I ask for a fresh portion of grace that will give me the strength I need to live and work with your character reflected in my own. And for whatever falls short, there is grace to cover that too.

What values define the way you live your life?

Light of Approval

Indeed, by faith our ancestors received approval.

HEBREWS 11:2 NRSV

In the light of your face, oh God, I see myself more clearly. It is by faith that I have been saved, not through anything I could have ever done. I could not talk my way into your favor. Your goodness is poured out over my life in abundant grace, not because I did anything to deserve it, but because I am yours. I am in relationship with you through faith.

Thank you, God, that this mystery is illustrated even in this very prayer. The very moment I turn to you in prayer, my faith is being exercised. There is nothing I could do to add or take away from what you've done; I couldn't talk you out of loving me. I won't stop turning to you, Lord; you are the best thing I've ever known. As I walk with you, fill me with your revelation-knowledge that reveals who you are and what you are up to. May my faith grow so that I may be closer to you. That's all that matters!

Are you trying to earn God's approval?

Contentment

I am not saying this because I am in need, for I have
learned to be content whatever the circumstances.

PHILIPPIANS 4:11 NIV

Holy One, you are the source of all life. Whatever I lack can
be found in you. You are the love I long for, the joy that
makes my heart sing. Whatever my life looks like right now,
whether my bank account is full or running low, or I am
grieving or celebrating, it is in you that I find everything I
need. When disappointment begins to creep in because
I've been comparing my life to those around me who
I think have "made it," wash your grace over my mind.
Then I will see with eyes that are clear not cloudy with
comparison.

I want to be able to echo the same sentiments as Paul did
when he said that he learned to be content whatever the
circumstances. I know that your values are different from
the world's, and as I grow into more of who I am in you,
your love settles the questions in my heart in every season.
I have everything I need for today. Let me be content with
what I have.

*Does your contentment change
based on your circumstances?*

No Need to Fear

I asked the LORD for help, and he answered me.
He saved me from all that I feared.

PSALM 34:4 NCV

God my peace, in you I find the rest I so desperately need.
You know my heart and the anxious thoughts that threaten
my peace. You know the fears that cause me to batten
down the hatches and react in ways that are not beneficial
for me or anyone else. I know that I can trust you. Fear is
a liar that makes the unknown feel impossibly difficult; but
you, God, give grace to those walking in the valleys and to
those on the mountaintops. All fear does is shut me down,
keeping me in a box that I have outgrown. I know that you
provide everything I need; I don't need to fear.

Even when I am afraid, I will trust you; I will walk into the
winds of the unknown, hand-in-hand with you. If things
get overwhelming, I know that you will save me. Above
all, I know that you are with me, and that you offer help
whenever I need it! Thank you that I am not on this path
alone even when I'm facing what I feared I never could, it
isn't as bad as I imagined. You are my saving grace, my
ever-present help.

What fears are keeping you from moving forward today?

your Will

"Your kingdom come.
Your will be done,
On earth as it is in heaven."

MATTHEW 6:10 NASB

God, as the days pass and they start to blend into one another, it is so easy for me to get caught up in my schedule. As the days turn into weeks and the weeks into months, if I am not taking intentional time with you, I find my heart growing more tuned toward my needs and wants. But you, oh God, are bigger than my little life. Your ways are better than my most calculated plans. Lord, I don't want to live a small life only concerned with my little area of the world.

I partner with you, God, that your ways would be manifest on the earth. May your will, your intentions, your desires, be fulfilled on the earth, just like they are in heaven. May my life be one of full submission and partnership with the King of kings, that your will would be done in my life, your kingdom come in the places I work and live. Give me eyes that see the vision of your love changing hearts and lives all around. I yield myself to you, knowing your plans are better than my own. What a privilege.

Is there room in your life for God to change your plans?

Not Helpless

When the righteous cry for help, the LORD hears
and delivers them out of all their troubles.

PSALM 34:17 ESV

God my help, there is no one in all the earth who is like you. You have delivered me from every trouble I have ever known. Even now, as I face the challenges of my life, I know that you are with me. You haven't left me yet, and you're not going to now. Your faithful love shows up time and again, delivering me from darkness into light.

Sometimes, when the dark night seems too long to take, it isn't until the light has come that I can see that you were there all along—even when I thought I had lost all hope. You haven't given up on me, so I won't give up on you. I know that no matter what comes, I am not helpless because you are on my side. You are my great deliverer; I will not fear the outcome. Surround me with your love once again, Lord. It is my comfort and the peace I so desperately need.

What help do you need today?

With Joy

Rejoice in the Lord always; again I will say, rejoice!

PHILIPPIANS 4:4 NASB

God of my great joy, you are wonderful. Right here, where my feet are planted, is where I will jump for joy, because you are good. When I look at my life, I see the mark of your mercy all over it. Your delight over me fills me with courage, and I can't help but rejoice over your great love. When I thought I had lost the ability to feel joy, when the dark night stretched into a dark season and the light of life felt like a distant memory, you led me out into an open space to rest. Slowly, as my heart opened to the light of your love, I felt its rays softening the hardness.

As my heart comes alive in you again, how could I not rejoice? I am so grateful that joy is not superficial; it reaches to the depths. It fills the deepest crevices of pain and flows into the cracks that seemed too deep to reach. How good you are, oh faithful one.

What joys are in your life right now?

Surrendered Mind

To set the mind on the flesh is death,
but to set the mind on the Spirit is life and peace.

ROMANS 8:6 NRSV

You are the Lord over every one of my days. Today, as I set my mind on you, let my thoughts be filled with your life and peace. I offer you the screen of my mind; I surrender my thoughts to you, asking that your Spirit would fill them with the fruit that only you give. When I walk into chaotic situations, may your perfect peace keep my mind steady. When I encounter others who are burdened by fear and shame, may the light of your love keep faith's flame ablaze in me. What does it matter if I lay down my life for you but keep my thoughts as my own without submission to you?

Lord, I know the best changes are those that happen from the inside out. I offer you my mind; when my thoughts start jumping to things that are neither helpful nor beneficial, redirect them. Help me to remember that your ways of life reach to every part. You can have it all, Lord.

How often do you notice the nature of what your thoughts reflect?

Repentance Matters

"Repent of your sins and turn to God,
for the Kingdom of Heaven is near."

MATTHEW 3:2 NLT

Merciful One, you are full of forgiveness. Thank you for your heart that is always bent on reconciliation, waiting for the opportunity to fold your children into your arms. Lord, you see how many times I choose my own desires over connection with you. I don't want to live in an unending cycle of selfishness and guilt that leads me to you.

Lord, you draw me in with your kindness. How could you be so patient with me? I see that my selfish ways lead to destruction of relationship, and I don't want that life. Forgive me of my sins, Lord; I turn away from them and turn toward you. God of love, I ask that you would fill me with your presence that gives me life. Thank you for your mercies that are new every day. You're never maxed-out on forgiveness. I am humbled by you, God, and I gladly submit to you today.

*Is there something that is keeping you
from connecting with God?*

Tempted

Let no one say when he is tempted,
"I am tempted by God";
for God cannot be tempted by evil,
nor does He Himself tempt anyone.

JAMES 1:13 NKJV

Lord, I believe that you are better than I've known. You do not tease your children or lead us into situations where we are forced to figure things out on our own. When you teach, you do it with grace. You don't throw your kids into the deep end of the pool when they haven't had any swimming lessons. Your kindness is our guide into truth.

Lord, where I have false beliefs about who you are and how you do things, would you reframe my mind? When I am tempted to sin, I know that you have no part in that except to provide a way out so that I may stand up under it. Your love lifts me, giving me courage to choose your ways even when the easy way out is staring me down. Your way of love is better; may I always choose to follow you on that path.

When you are tempted, what can help you resist?

Not My Home

Stop imitating the ideals and opinions of the culture around you, but be inwardly transformed by the Holy Spirit through a total reformation of how you think. This will empower you to discern God's will as you live a beautiful life, satisfying and perfect in his eyes.

ROMANS 12:2 TPT

Jehovah, as I live a life submitted to you, keep me aware of the difference between your kingdom's ways and the ways of the world around me. Let me be a learner of the culture of your kingdom, living out the values that supersede the wisdom of the world. I don't want to be a theological anthropologist; I want to be an active participant, a citizen of heaven releasing the fruit of the Spirit that gives life to all who seek it. A beautiful life is one lived in submission and partnership with you and your ways. I will remember that this life is temporary; this earthly dwelling, as it is, will not be my home forever.

When I think about eternity, daring to grasp what that could look like, why would I choose to limit my life to one enmeshed in society's standards of importance? Let me live in the overflow of the abundance of all that you give, and I will freely live and give in the same way.

When you consider how short this life is, how does that make you rethink your priorities?

Selfish Ambition

"Whoever exalts himself will be humbled,
and whoever humbles himself will be exalted."

MATTHEW 23:12 ESV

Father, when I struggle to lay down my own desires and preferences, keep my heart tuned to your voice that keeps me in-check. It is my inclination to surround myself with those who value the same things I do and who think the same way, but that is not how your kingdom works. You set us in family, which means that we belong to one another while all being very different. Lord, I know that humility is necessary in relationship—in any successful one. May my heart remain tactile, sensitive to your touch, and may I value relationship with others over getting my own way. Lord, where I tend to isolate myself because it's easier, draw me out into relationship where I will find my true place in family.

Thank you for your example, Jesus. You humbled yourself more than anyone else ever could. You set the standard, and I will not try to pave my own path, fooling myself into thinking that it is a holier way. There is nothing holier than following your example. Help me to choose humility instead of my own selfish ambition.

*Is getting your way more important than unity
with the Spirit and others?*

April

You will call on me
and come and pray to me,
and I will listen to you.

JEREMIAH 29:12 NIV

No Criticism

Keep a good conscience so that in the thing in which
you are slandered, those who revile your good behavior
in Christ will be put to shame.

1 PETER 3:16 NASB

Lord, may everything I do be done with excellence for your
kingdom's sake. As I labor in love, following your example,
may my eyes stay fixed on you, not on what others are
saying about me. Jesus, when you lived and ministered
to the lowly and broken, you did not escape the criticism
of those who thought they knew better. May I remember
when people say things about me that aren't true, that you
endured slander and so can I. May it not cause me to give
up, but may I be filled with encouragement that I am walking
in your ways and you can handle the backlash for me.

As long as I am doing what I do with a pure and loving
heart, I will keep a clear conscience and run the race that I
am in. No critic can dictate the value of my life or offering.
Keep me tucked into your side when the arrows fly, so I
won't be taken out before my time. I'm doing this with and
for you, God, not for accolades or acceptance from others.

How do you react to criticism?

Prone to Wander

Lord, I know that people's lives are not their own;
it is not for them to direct their steps.

JEREMIAH 10:23 NIV

All-knowing One, you alone see the scope of my life—the end from the beginning. As I journey with you, choosing paths to walk and ways to turn, my comfort is in knowing that you are with me every single step. Even when I wander from your ways, you are there. There is nowhere I could go where you are not. There is no path I could tread that is unfamiliar to you. Even so, this life is not my own. Direct my steps so that no matter the twists or turns the road may take, it leads me to your kingdom in the end.

I trust you, Lord; you are the ultimate guide. You have all the wisdom I could ever need. Fill me anew, today with the power of your presence. In this very moment I know that I have not wandered beyond your mercy. Thank you for your grace that empowers me to press into you when I want to run away. You are good. Break down every lie that says otherwise.

When you feel far from where you think you should be, what gives you hope?

You Are Perfect

As for God, His way is perfect;
The word of the LORD is proven;
He is a shield to all who trust in Him.

PSALM 18:30 NKJV

Lord, you are more than I can try to describe. When I feel the lack in my life, I remember the fullness of who you are, the perfection of your ways. Your love draws me in; it doesn't push me away with intimidation tactics. You know that it is kindness that draws people. Of course you know that. You designed us to be like you. You cover me as I trust in you. You hem me in, behind and before, keeping me from stumbling. Your Word is alive, breathing courage and passion into the most destitute souls. Who can describe your goodness? Who can recount the ways you have faithfully saved your people?

You are constantly reaching out, not withholding any good thing that would benefit your children. You pour out your love so we can drink deeply and become just like you. I ask for fresh revelation of your greatness today, Lord. Shine your light in a way I haven't seen before.

What are the best attributes you have seen
God exhibit in your life?

Source of Hope

I pray that God, the source of hope, will fill you completely with joy and peace because you trust in him. Then you will overflow with confident hope through the power of the Holy Spirit.

ROMANS 15:13 NLT

God, my source, in you is all I need. When life requires more than I have to give, I feel the trickle of my stored-up hope draining. In you is plenty. I come to drink today of your goodness. I need to be filled up. Like a vessel that is running low, I stand under the waters of your love and am filled once again. The presence of your Spirit fills me with the peace I long for—peace that is my sense of home. Your joy infuses my heart with life: the life I need. When you fill me, there isn't just enough to top me off; you don't ration your love.

May I overflow with hope that is confident in your strong love to carry out every promise you have ever spoken. I don't conjure up hope out of thin air; wishful thinking gets me nowhere. But you, Lord, are a living hope-giver, filling me with tangible confidence that comes from your Spirit. Thank you for the power of your presence that operates out of the abundance of your incredible character.

What are you hoping for today?

Desiring Humility

The reward for humility and fear of the LORD
is riches and honor and life.

PROVERBS 22:4 ESV

Lord, when I seek you with all my heart, I find you. You are not hiding in an obscure part of the earth; I don't have to go on a pilgrimage to find you. I find you right here, in the middle of my joy and my mess. The life I long for is not to be found in the next thing. I won't find satisfaction in the nostalgic memories of my past. Right here is where I will find what I long for, in the working out of my faith in the nitty-gritty parts of life.

I choose you today, Lord. I humble myself before you, laying down my longings and ambitions at the feet of your mercy, knowing that you alone are the one who can satisfy me. As I go about my day with you in mind, I know I will find you in places I wouldn't think to look twice on my own. I offer myself to you in every moment. May my mind continually turn to you today.

*What does submission to God, in humility,
look like to you?*

Cannot Be Lost

Every valley shall be raised up,
every mountain and hill made low;
the rough ground shall become level,
the rugged places a plain.

ISAIAH 40:4 NIV

Mighty One, I have placed all my bets on you. I have sunk all my savings into knowing you; don't let me down now! I am continually laying down my life before you as I seek to follow your ways. I know the road won't be straight and smooth; it certainly hasn't been up until now. But I also know that your love sustains me in ways I never imagined it could. Level the rough places and make the jagged paths into open spaces. Just when it seems like the storm is too much to bear, speak peace and shine your light, bringing out all that was hidden.

I will not give up, no matter what may come, when I am linked to you. You will keep me when the way is winding, never letting me be lost. In your time, God, lead me out in peace. Wherever I am, let me be found in you.

Do you believe God is with you in your life right now?

Renew My Mind

Let the Spirit renew your thoughts and attitudes.

EPHESIANS 4:23 NLT

Spirit of God, I long for your river of life to rush through me. I am open to you. Come fill me with your love that washes away every fear and clears out every stuck part. Renew my mind today with your peace that clears the clutter of jumbled thoughts. You are the one I long for; I know that when you speak, you bring life. Where there have been thoughts of despair and hopelessness, replace them with hope that comes from you and the life you bring.

I wait on you now, God. I will not rush on with my day until you meet with me here in this present moment. Renew my attitudes, so instead of dread I would be filled with peace to face any situation. I cannot do this on my own, Lord. Do the work that only you can do. You are more than welcome to shift everything that stands against you and your kingdom within me. Here I am; have your way!

What thoughts and attitudes reflect the character of God?

Made to Be

Since we have gifts that differ according to the grace given to us, each of us is to exercise them accordingly.

ROMANS 12:6 NASB

Lord, you are so creative. You made me uniquely to reflect your image. No two people are the same, and I am grateful to know that I was never meant to be a carbon copy of someone else. Thank you for your love that deposits incredible gifts in each person in different ways. I will not despise what you have put in me in favor of what I admire in others. Help me to shine brightly, living with full intention and freedom to operate in the gifts that you have so generously given me. As I grow in my knowledge of who you are, I grow in confidence of who you have made me to be.

Why would I want to be anyone else when you took the time and attention to purposefully make me just as I am, even with all the quirks? I offer you my gifts, Lord, and I will live using them for the increase of your kingdom on the earth.

What are you good at doing that doesn't come as easily to others?

Wise Enough

If any of you is lacking in wisdom,
ask God, who gives to all generously and ungrudgingly,
and it will be given you.

JAMES 1:5 NRSV

All-knowing One, I know that you have all the answers that I'm looking for. God of wisdom, you give guidance to all who ask. Your advice isn't cheap; you don't give pat answers that don't actually help. Your Word is full of wisdom. May I have an open heart to hear what you would say, especially when it costs me something.

Jesus, when I look at your life that you lived in wisdom, it doesn't look like what I know to be smart choices. However, the world's wisdom isn't the same as yours. I trust that your ways are better; your example is more fruitful than logic. You are the way, the truth, and the life, and I will follow you. There is no one more qualified to weigh in on my life than you who created it. Even so, may I receive your wisdom when I recognize it in the counsel of those around me. Speak, Lord, I am listening.

What areas do you need God's wisdom for right now?

Willing Submission

Obey your leaders and act under their authority. They
are watching over you, because they are responsible
for your souls. Obey them so that they will do this work
with joy, not sadness. It will not help you
to make their work hard.

HEBREWS 13:17 NCV

Great God, fill me anew today with the fresh wind of
your grace, blowing away all the dust of days before. You
speak, and my heart takes courage. I intentionally lay my
heart open before you; fill me with the knowledge of your
goodness and great care. Draw me near to you, that I may
take courage in being found in you. Help me to serve the
leaders in my life with a humble heart, submitting to them
even when I disagree with their decisions. Give me grace
to remember that when I lead, I do the best I can, and my
leaders are doing the same.

I willingly submit myself not only to your leadership but
to theirs as well, knowing nothing goes unseen by you.
Everything done in love is not wasted, and I choose love
over my own preferences. Thank you for your grace that
covers me.

Who can you submit to rather than fight against today?

Self-Discipline

We have all of these great witnesses who encircle us like clouds. So we must let go of every wound that has pierced us and the sin we so easily fall into. Then we will be able to run life's marathon race with passion and determination, for the path has been already marked out before us.

HEBREWS 12:1 TPT

Mighty God, I invite your perfect presence to meet me where I am today. I don't pretend to be in a place that I'm not. I'm not going to try to convince myself that I've got it all together; if only that were true! But, no, you don't require perfection. You don't even require that I be in a good place. Thank you that you accept me just as I am: faults, failings, and all.

Lord, I will not forget that others have gone before me, and still others are on their own journeys of faith with you. None of these paths are without obstacles or pain. I will not fool myself into thinking that I am alone in my struggles. Instead, I ask for the grace to let go of things I can't control, leave behind the sin that tries to sidetrack me, and trust that you will heal me as I walk the path of forgiveness. I am so grateful for your presence and for the power found in you.

What do you need to let go of today?

Real Future

Come now, you who say, "Today or tomorrow we will go to such and such a town and spend a year there, doing business and making money." Yet you do not even know what tomorrow will bring. What is your life? For you are a mist that appears for a little while and then vanishes. Instead you ought to say, "If the LORD wishes, we will live and do this or that."

JAMES 4:13–15 NRSV

Lord, keeper of my thoughts, you know every plan that takes root in my heart. My tendency to set my hope in the goals I set may get me going, but true hope is only found in you. Lord, may I live with a loose grasp on the plans I set, knowing that whether they happen or not, you have good things in store. Thank you that my future is much brighter than any I could ever dream up because it will belong to you and your kingdom.

As I walk through this life, I pray that I will find pleasure in your goodness that does not change based on circumstances. No matter whether all my dreams come true or every plan I have falls apart, you do not change. You are better than all my desires put together. Help me to believe that to the very core of my being. Have your way, God.

If your plans fail, where does the hope of your future lie?

Present

No one has ever seen God.
But if we love each other, God lives in us,
and his love is brought to full expression in us.

1 JOHN 4:12 NLT

Ever-present One, you are the full expression of love. Wherever there is love that lays down offenses, there you are. Where there is love that chooses to express itself in kindness rather than manipulation, there you are again. I may not know what your features look like, but I know you in your character. Give me deeper revelation-knowledge of your presence as I look for signs of you in my life. You don't complicate matters, you simplify them. I know I will find you when I look for you; I see you at work in families healing and communities rallying around their members.

May I be a vessel of your love, being made more like you, even as I seek to know you. As I look to you, let me resemble the goodness of my Father more and more until the days run out and you have come again. I long for that day, but in the meantime I choose to live out your ways, not my own!

*Where do you see God's love at work
in the lives of those around you?*

Still Promised

"For I know the plans I have for you," declares the Lord,
"plans to prosper you and not to harm you,
plans to give you hope and a future."

JEREMIAH 29:11 NIV

Lord, I cling to your promise that your plans for me are good. When life throws me a curveball and I am left reeling from its impact, remind me that this is not the end. There is no time limit to your grace; you don't set an expiration date on mercy's freshness. My plans may be thrown off course, and even thrown out the window, but yours have not changed. What a hope!

I trust you, God. You keep me on the path of life until I reach the end of mine. I will not give up or give in. As long as I have you, I have everything that matters. Keep me steady when I start to tremble. Keep me going when I feel like my feet are as heavy as lead. Keep me, just keep me. I take hope and courage, while clinging to you, in your good plans for my life—the life that you see clearly. Though it looks different than I'd hoped, here I am, Lord. Lead me on.

Is your hope in your own plans or in God's goodness?

Jealousy

Wrath is fierce and anger is a flood,
But who can stand before jealousy?

PROVERBS 27:4 NASB

Merciful God, you are not prone to anger. You are rich in love, patient in extending mercy. When I consider all that your kingdom holds for those who love you, I am encouraged to keep going in you. Help me keep my eyes fixed on you, the author and finisher of my faith. Keep me from getting distracted by the details of other people's lives. May I not give into the temptation to compare the current state of my journey with the highlights of others'. There is no timeline for success, and what does success matter if I lose my peace with you in the process?

Keep my heart from jealousy that acts out of suspicion and resentment. What a slippery slope. May my heart be satisfied in you, Lord, and may I stay with resolute vision on the path laid before me. Thank you for your grace.

Has envy kept you from enjoying what you have?

My Reconciliation

If while we were enemies we were reconciled to God by the death of his Son, much more, now that we are reconciled, shall we be saved by his life.

ROMANS 5:10 ESV

Redeemer, you are the source of my salvation. In you, Jesus, I find freedom from the chains of sin, from every detrimental cycle of shame that leads to death. In your life, I find my own life. You breathe your breath of renewal in me and I'm like a new person! It is too much for my mind to understand that you have made a way for me to know you in death and life. It's a marvelous mystery. You end conflicts and make enemies into friends. Who else is there like you?

May all the earth know that you are the great liberator; you set the captives free and give them a hope and a future. Those who have found their freedom in you are set on pathways of peace. You lead them into a life of liberty from the inside out. Who can hold someone accountable to the state of their heart? Only you. And what a wonderful work you do in bringing life to dark and dead places. I once was dead in my sin but look at what you've done. I'm alive in you.

How has your relationship with Jesus changed your life?

Beauty in Pain

"In the same way I will not cause pain
without allowing something new to be born,"
says the Lord.
"If I cause you the pain,
I will not stop you from giving birth
to your new nation," says your God.

ISAIAH 66:9 NCV

God of comfort, you meet me in the darkness of my pain. When it all seems too much to bear, you show up and lighten the load. Lord, take what is broken and make it whole in you. You are the master restorer. Take the agonizing pain of my grief and suffering and cause something beautiful to come out of it. In the midst of it, I can't imagine that it would even be worth it. Even so, I hold onto hope that this won't be in vain.

I believe, Lord; help my unbelief. You are an expert at creating beauty out of messes. I wouldn't put it past you that this present suffering would produce something worth marveling at. Let it be so. Even when that thought doesn't bring me comfort, I will cling to you. You are with me, right in the middle of my anguish.

*Can you see beauty that came out of
painful times in your life?*

Already Won

"The Lord your God is the one who goes with you to fight for you against your enemies to give you victory."

DEUTERONOMY 20:4 NIV

Mighty God, you are the victorious one. You have conquered sin and death. What could now stand in your way? When I look at my present troubles, I will remember that you have taken on greater situations, and you always come out the victor.

I won't be afraid. I cling to you in faith, knowing you've got it all under control. You haven't lost your touch, and you aren't worried. As I look to my side and see you there, I am filled with confidence. I know that with you I don't have to wonder if I'll make it out alive. You have got me, safe and secure. God, I won't move from your side. You are the one I get all my security from. Thank you for fighting for me. I would wither from fear without you. With you by my side, I am confident in your ability to fight as well as care for me at the same time.

What battles are you tired of fighting on your own?

Carrying Enough

"What does it profit them if they gain the whole world, but lose or forfeit themselves?"

LUKE 9:25 NRSV

God of all my days, you see every dream locked inside my heart. You know every longing and every desire. You see the purely motivated and those that serve my own interests. Thank you for honoring my heart. As I journey with you in this life, I pray that my heart would stay soft toward you. May I never grow cold with the selfishness of sin that causes me to act without compassion and react out of fear. What a miserable way to live.

What would I gain if I had all the success I ever dreamed, but lived with a cold, angry heart? If I lost my connection with you, choosing my own interests over the way of love, I would be at a disadvantage. Lord, keep me close to you, so that I may respond to your love at every turn. There is nothing like the fruit that comes from living a life connected to you.

What motivations are driving your goals?

Defeat Is Impossible

Then you will prosper, if you take care to fulfill the
statutes and judgments with which the LORD charged
Moses concerning Israel. Be strong and of good
courage; do not fear nor be dismayed.

1 CHRONICLES 22:13 NKJV

God my Father, you are the leader of my life. May I never
walk away from your wisdom that brings life. As long
as my life is joined to yours, I will taste the fruit of your
kingdom, carrying it with me into every situation. I will
not be dismayed when the timing of your promises does
not match up with my own. Encourage my heart when
disappointment starts to set in. Keep my heart woven into
yours, giving me the strength and courage I need to keep
going.

Walking in the confidence of who you are, I will find the
satisfaction I'm looking for. How could I miss it, when it's all
based in you? Your strength becomes my own as I lean on
you. I don't have to trust in my own abilities. What a relief!
Thank you for your grace that leads me into the abundance
of life in you.

*What unknown outcomes are keeping you
from showing up with courage?*

As I Know It

This world and its desires are in the process
of passing away, but those who love to do the will
of God live forever.

1 JOHN 2:17 TPT

Lord, when I consider the works of your hands, when I look
around me and see your wonderful creation, I can't help
but marvel at your creativity. I also can't help but notice
the decay of the earth; this world won't last forever as
is. It's changing every day, and so am I. You are the only
being that does not ever change. You are consistent in
your goodness, always offering the fruit of your kingdom
to those who are joined to you. The longer I walk this earth,
the wearier I am of the world's priorities and its ways. The
only thing that truly matters is the life that you offer.

Your lavish love is astounding; it can't be measured! It will
lead us into your everlasting kingdom that will never show
any signs of wear. It will not be overcome, and it will not
decay. Thank you for an eternal hope, Lord.

*When this life has you discouraged, do you
take hope that there is a better life in store?*

Matching Wisdom

"With God are wisdom and might;
he has counsel and understanding."

JOB 12:13 ESV

All-knowing One, your advice is always spot-on. The wisdom of your counsel is full of incredible insight; you always have the best solution for any problem that arises. Your understanding is unmatched. How could it be when you are the source of everything that exists? I won't waste my time on trying to buy wisdom from experts. Though there is wisdom in seeking out many counselors, you are my go-to. I will weigh all other advice against yours.

God, you see the situations in my life that look like big question marks to me. I don't know which direction to go or what path to take. Give me the guidance I need to choose the path that will be full of life and let me be freely who I am, growing into your likeness more and more. I know that with you as my guide, I can't be steered wrong.

What do you need wisdom for right now?

Each Holy Act

Pursue peace with everyone, and the holiness without which no one will see the Lord.

HEBREWS 12:14 NRSV

Holy God, you are the great peacemaker. Everything you do is sown in kindness and compassion. Your ways are perfect and your character is unmatched. Lord, I want to be just like you, reflecting your goodness to all who look at my life. May I live my life in purity of purpose, walking hand-in-hand with you down the path of love that leads to your kingdom.

When I am tempted to brush off grudges of offense as being justified, remind me that the pursuit of peace is your better way. I don't want to live in the twisted ways of self-righteousness. As I align myself with your character, I find that humility is the key to living a life of your kind of laid-down love that puts others' well-being above its own. What a way to live. Give me grace to be like you, Jesus. It's what I want.

What does holiness look like in your life?

It Will Be Done

I also persevered in the work on this wall,
and we acquired no land, and all my servants were
gathered there for the work.

NEHEMIAH 5:16 ESV

All-sufficient One, fill me with the courage of your love that enables me to thrive in every circumstance. Give me perseverance to follow through on what I have to do. Sometimes it seems like too much. When the work is never-ending, and the demands are great, give me the persistence I need to do what I can and the grace to let go of what I can't. I know that as I work, day-by-day, projects will be finished.

Other things are harder to measure, but let your grace remain the same. I know that if I will not give up, what needs to get done will be accomplished. In a go-go-go world with tons of distractions, the extremes feel personified. I ask for your grace to be faithful in my commitments and to be as diligent in letting myself rest at the end of the day. I need your help in this, Lord.

*Are you feeling the pressure of work
that seems never-ending?*

Born of Pain

"This is My commandment, that you love one another, just as I have loved you."

JOHN 15:12 NASB

Merciful God, your love is unmatched in its tenacity. It pursues at all costs, flooding all those in its path with its wonderful, life-giving properties. There is no expiration date on the effects of your affection. You don't call us to a lifestyle that you did not live first; your example of loyal love is the measure that we set our lives against. Your commandment that we love each other the way that we have been loved by you is only possible through your grace that empowers us. You set the bar high, Jesus. I see in my own life how short I fall of your devoted love.

Thank you for grace that covers the many times I fail in this, and thank you for the example that I have to look to. Your love never fails, of that I am sure. May I look like you in the way I love the people around me.

What does it mean to love like Jesus?

Beautiful Reflection

One thing I ask from the LORD, this only do I seek:
that I may dwell in the house of the LORD
all the days of my life,
to gaze on the beauty of the LORD
and to seek him in his temple.

PSALM 27:4 NIV

Holy One, you are the one I live for. As I seek after you with all my heart, the desire to know you grows ever stronger. I am so grateful for relationship, that I can know you and follow you all the days of my life. Lord, I ask for a fresh revelation of your beauty. I want to see you in a way I've never seen you before. Fill my heart with the knowledge of your goodness. There is nothing that you give out of your generous heart of love that ends up being meaningless. You are full of so much grace and goodness, I could never take it all.

Lord, may my life be a beautiful reflection of your life within mine. Your ways are perfect, and you are making me more like you by the day. I'm so grateful. Keep it coming until I stand with you in your forever kingdom.

How is the life of Jesus reflected in your life?

My Safety

They will not be disgraced in hard times;
even in famine they will have more than enough.

PSALM 37:19 NLT

Rock of Salvation, you are the refuge my soul longs for. I stand on your foundation of peace that keeps me steady no matter what is going on around me. I am always connected to your abundant grace that empowers me with everything I need. I know you will provide for me when resources are running thin; you won't leave me hanging. You never do. When I walk through hard times, you will lead me out. They won't last forever. Even in the middle of them, you give me everything I need to survive. You're so good in your provision. I could never exhaust your reserves. What good news!

You are so reliable, Lord, why would I look anywhere else for the help I need when you freely give it? You are so rich in love and mercy. Your peace is my portion in every season. Joy dwells deep within me, connected to your fountains of life. I am so grateful for your friendship. You are the best.

Where do you find your security in hard times?

Accept the Waiting

"Then you will call upon Me and go and pray to Me,
and I will listen to you."

JEREMIAH 29:12 NKJV

Prince of Peace, you are the portion I need for my day. You fill me with the provision of your affection that carries me through every bump and turn that I encounter along my path. You never fail, Lord. When I am afraid, I will call on you. When I don't know where to turn, I face you. When I don't know what to do, I will trust you. I know that as I look to you, I will be filled with the confidence I need to keep going. You fill me with courage when I pray for help. I know that no matter what, you are with me.

Why would I run away when your steady presence is the calm I so desperately long for? I won't run, Lord, except into you! I will leave the timing to you, and I will learn to rest in the waiting. May my heart find its respite in you.

How does waiting make you feel?

Thankful in Trials

My brothers and sisters, whenever you face trials of
any kind, consider it nothing but joy, because you know
that the testing of your faith produces endurance; and
let endurance have its full effect, so that you may be
mature and complete, lacking in nothing.

JAMES 1:2-4 NRSV

God, you are an ever-present help in time of trouble. Look
at my life, and see what I am up against. I can't pretend
I don't have concerns. But, Lord, when I look at your
Word, I am reminded of the fruit that comes from facing
trials. I will not despair for the troubles I am experiencing,
knowing that no one is immune to hard times. Your grace
is sufficient in each and every one. Let me endure the tests
of my faith with the joy of foresight that sees that pressure
produces beautiful treasures. Without intense pressure and
times of darkness, there wouldn't be gems of many kinds,
including diamonds.

When I am walking through the darkness of a trial, may I
remember that the most precious treasures are created in
those situations. I yield to you even now, asking for your
heavenly perspective to help me through.

What can you be thankful for in the trial you are facing?

Where you Are

> "Where two or three are gathered in my name,
> there am I among them."
>
> MATTHEW 18:20 ESV

Ever-present One, you are my rock-steady companion in life. There is no one quite like you; you're exceedingly faithful to those you love. Who can take away what you give? The gift of your presence is beautiful. I love to gather with others who love you. When I pray with others, I sense your grace and comfort in a way that's different than on my own. I have known the beauty of your comfort in the privacy of my pain; I have also felt your comfort in the company of others, and there's no way to describe the depth of the meaning it holds.

Your presence is always with your people. What a powerful reminder. A cord of three strands cannot be easily broken; even though we could go it alone with you, it's always better to journey together. The support of a good friend is incredible medicine. I certainly can't be my own friend, and that's not how you designed it. I'm grateful for companionship in spirit and in body.

Who encourages you in your faith?

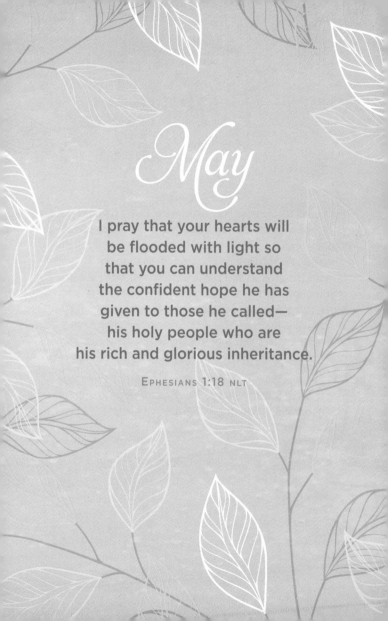

May

I pray that your hearts will
be flooded with light so
that you can understand
the confident hope he has
given to those he called—
his holy people who are
his rich and glorious inheritance.

EPHESIANS 1:18 NLT

A Glimpse

Surely there is a future,
And your hope will not be cut off.

PROVERBS 23:18 NASB

God of all my days, in you is my hope. In the midst of challenges, I need the reminder that the story isn't finished; you're not done with me yet. I believe that where you are is where I find the strength I need to keep going. When I'm tempted to give up and call it quits, fill me with your grace that empowers me to cling to you. When circumstances move and shake my life, I realize that you are the only sure thing I have. Keep me steady in your love and give me eyes of faith that see the future that my weary mind cannot dream up.

You are my portion, Lord, and you are more than enough. You both strengthen and satisfy. Breathe your life into me again today, reviving my soul to catch a glimpse of the goodness in store for me.

What hope do you have for the future?

Captives Set Free

We have freedom now, because Christ made us free.
So stand strong. Do not change and go back into the
slavery of the law.

GALATIANS 5:1 NCV

Redeemer, you are the chain-breaking freedom fighter
for every soul. Your lavish love fueled your journey on this
earth, clothed in flesh and bones. Jesus, thank you for the
sacrifice of your life, and even more that it didn't stop at
death. You rose again, defeating the grave and setting
us free from sin and shame. Let me stand strong on the
foundation of your love, not going back to a life dictated
by rules that don't bring life. May your resurrection life and
power be the moving force of my life whenever I get stuck,
remembering I am not a slave to the fear that would keep
me captive.

I am free because you set me free. May I never go back to
living with the limitations that keep love from spreading. I
look to you, my victorious one, as the example of the life I
want to live; may I not be small-minded or cold-hearted.

*Are you living bound to the law, or are you living
in the freedom that Christ offers?*

All I Carry

"The foreigner residing among you must be treated as your native-born. Love them as yourself, for you were foreigners in Egypt. I am the LORD your God."

LEVITICUS 19:34 NIV

Lord over all, you exhibit love to everyone equally, not picking and choosing favorites. God, give me a heart that is undivided in its love for you and for others. May my own biases come crashing down as I live with your love clothing my heart and mind. I am grateful to be found in you, fully accepted. How could I turn away those who are different than me, excusing it because of fear? Your love kicks fear out of the door; there's no excuse to trade compassion for suspicion.

Lord, as you are benevolent to everyone without preference, let me be like you. I can only give what I have received, so refresh me in your love today that pushes out every fear. Thank you for your love that is all-inclusive. Father, may I operate as your child in the goodness of your character to all, dealing in mercy and grace.

Is fear keeping you from loving others
who are different than you?

Enemies Will See

"Blessed are those who are persecuted for
righteousness' sake, for theirs is
the kingdom of heaven."

MATTHEW 5:10 NKJV

Savior, there is no way to measure the length of the love
that you send as a lifeline to everyone who calls on you.
Your faithful grace sustains those who face harassment
and bullying for your sake. Though they are mistreated
and suffer for your name, you say that they will receive a
reward that moth and rust cannot destroy. Lord, when I am
discouraged by the troubles I face, may I remember that
there are those being beaten and put to death because of
their faith in you. In comparison, my problems seem minor.

Lord, may I stand with those who are suffering for your
sake; if I face the same kind of persecution, I pray that I
will endure it with love and mercy. May the enemies of
your kingdom see for themselves the lengths that you go
for your people. Give them eyes to see your love so their
hearts will turn to you.

Have you suffered for the sake of the Gospel?

Within the Walls

"Peace be within your walls,
and security within your towers."

PSALM 122:7 NRSV

Mighty One, you are my strong tower—the one I run to for refuge in times of trouble. You keep me settled with peace as the atmosphere within my home. I invite you into the dwelling of my heart. Keep me safe and secure, wrapped in the warmth of your mighty love. I know that there is no need to fear, for you are with me. You are the defender of my soul. Nothing can destroy my heart with you as its guard. Even when storms are raging around me, I will experience your rest. I will sleep peacefully, knowing I am taken care of.

I trust that your keen eye sees everything that would dare sneak into the camp of my heart; keep me alert as I rest in you. I know that even when an enemy comes into the camp, I have everything I need to confidently deal with it. You are with me, my peace giver, and I dwell in the security that your love brings.

When is the last time you felt peace in the middle of chaos?

Inside Out

"Don't judge by his appearance or height, for I have rejected him. The LORD doesn't see things the way you see them. People judge by outward appearance, but the LORD looks at the heart."

1 SAMUEL 16:7 NLT

All-knowing One, you see right to the core of my heart. You see straight to the center of every matter, and details are laid plain before you. Though I look at people and judge them by what I see them do or say, and even sometimes how they look, this is not how you deal with people. The outward means nothing if it does not reflect the inner world. Lord, you look at motivations, not outward actions as the measure. You see a heart's intentions more clearly than I see the chair I'm sitting in.

Lord, let me be quick to give space for a person's character to shine through, slow to judge the obvious physical appearance. As you do, may I look deeper, past the surface, into a person's true worth which is not what a first-glance would dictate. Thank you for radically loving me beyond what can be quickly judged. You are so much better than anyone I've ever known.

How do you judge a person's worth?

When We Doubt

Keep being compassionate to those
who still have doubts.

JUDE 1:22 TPT

God, your kindness knows no limits. Your unending love does not give up on anyone. Walking this road long enough with you, times of doubt are almost inevitable; it is your faithful love, and the compassion of your people, that keeps me coming back to you. Your kind character never wavers; you are steadfast. Your love is strong enough to handle the doubts that may arise. There's no need to try to ignore them or cover them up. In the wondering, you faithfully meet me. You don't want me to pretend to be in a spiritual place that I'm not, and you are not bothered by the questions forced by the reality of my pain.

Lord, help me to remember that questioning is a part of the journey of life; keep me secure in your love as I learn what it means to press into healing. I trust you to not give up on me even when I give up on myself. And when I am strong in faith, walking in confidence, may your tender compassion keep my heart soft and patient with those around me in their own questioning.

Do you believe that it's okay to have doubts or questions?

Fear No Evil

Even though I walk through the valley
of the shadow of death,
I fear no evil, for You are with me;
Your rod and Your staff, they comfort me.

PSALM 23:4 NASB

Good Shepherd, I am living under your leadership; I know that you take care of me. I won't be afraid of what may come because you are by my side, guiding me in this life. Your constant presence is my comfort and my peace; no one can take you away from me. You keep your eye out for me, so I know that it doesn't matter what the path looks like. You've got me. Lord, when I walk through grief and suffering, draw me closer to your side. When I can't make the steps on my own, carry me, my good leader. I know that it's not too much to ask; it's what you gladly do.

Lord, you know my heart and how difficult it is for me to ask for the help I need. Would you answer the deepest needs of my heart with the lavish love and care that you are known for? I wouldn't want to do this life without you. You are the source of every good and perfect gift I've ever known. Keep me close, my God, with the confidence that there is nothing to fear when you are near.

*How does God's presence affect
your level of fear and anxiety?*

My Inspiration

All Scripture is given by inspiration of God,
and is profitable for doctrine, for reproof, for correction,
for instruction in righteousness.

2 TIMOTHY 3:16 NKJV

Holy One, guide me in your truth today. I look to you, finding nuggets of wisdom and revelation in your Word. They inspire me to dive deep into knowing you more. How I long for you. You have all the answers to questions I don't even know how to form. In you is the wisdom I am so desperate for; you have the keys to life. Even in correction, my soul is encouraged because your faithfulness reveals your good intentions for me.

There is no end to the revelation of your love. Fill me anew today with your thoughts that are too wonderful for me to make up. Your creativity knows no limitations. As I meditate on your Word, I ask that you would bring it alive in a new way. Thank you for your breath of life that puts animation to words that would otherwise fall flat. You are the speaker of life. In you I find who I am meant to be. I love you, Lord.

How does God's Word inspire you?

All I Am

"Love the LORD your God with all your heart,
all your soul, and all your strength."

DEUTERONOMY 6:5 NCV

Yahweh, in you is the fullness of life. I can't begin to imagine the extent of your goodness toward me, though I try. You don't withhold any part of you from your people, so why would I hold back from you? With all I am and all I have—my heart, my soul, and my strength—I offer you all the love I have to give. You loved me first, and still you love me to life. I am so grateful for the incredible way you pour out your grace on my life. I could never earn the love you so freely give. It's my turn to pour out my love on you.

Today, I choose to honor you with every part of me. Let my mind be filled with the fruit of your wisdom, my heart be filled with the joy that knowing you brings, and my body be filled with the strength that grace gives to do everything set before me—all for you. You can have every part of my life. I won't hold back from you.

*Is there any part of you that you've been
holding back from God?*

you Get Me

We do not have a high priest who is unable to empathize with our weaknesses, but we have one who has been tempted in every way, just as we are—yet he did not sin.

HEBREWS 4:15 NIV

Son of God, you are the hope of my heart. Knowing that you walked this earth and are acquainted with temptation, weakness, and suffering, I fully put my trust in you today. I don't have to pretend to be better than I am; I don't need to be "fine." You know, Jesus, the struggles that are so common in this life. You faced them all, and yet you did not fall into the trap of sin. Lord, I am reminded today that weakness is not failure; it is a part of being human. When my strength is waning, may I look to you. Your power is always available, ready to flow into those who are plugged into you.

Lord, let me remember that I don't succeed alone. I'm not meant to pull myself up by the bootstraps to make it through. Jesus, you leaned into the Father when your strength was going, and I will do the same by your Spirit.

What does it mean to you that God is familiar with your suffering?

Whole Again

The LORD is close to the brokenhearted;
he rescues those whose spirits are crushed.

PSALM 34:17 NLT

Faithful Father, you are close to the brokenhearted. You do not distance yourself from those in pain; you draw close to them in your peaceful presence. You rescue those whose hopes have been dashed and who cannot stand on their own two feet. You care for the weak, holding their grieving hearts with your tender arms. You are not far away. When my heart is raw with complex emotions, draw me into your comforting arms of grace.

When discouragement threatens to take the light out of my eyes, come close and surround me with your peaceful presence. You are the master restorer, making all things new. You don't return me to the way I was before pain became my teacher; you fill the cracks with your liquid love that shines like gold, making what was broken beautifully whole in you. What a glorious mystery. Come even closer, Lord. I need you.

What broken parts of your life need the Lord's restoration?

Sensitivity

Rejoice with those who rejoice,
weep with those who weep.

ROMANS 12:15 NRSV

God of love, you are so multi-faceted. Your light shines for all to see, and it meets every one of us right where we are. Thank you for your love that crosses every boundary; nothing can keep us from it. Lord, I have known your comfort in my time of need. I have known your incredible joy in times of celebration. You are not deaf to the various situations we find ourselves in. As you meet each one of us in our realities, let me be the same with empathy as my covering. Help me to be sensitive to the people around me, sharing in their joys and in their heartbreak.

You set us in families on purpose, Lord, that we would carry each other's burdens. A shared load is not as heavy as lugging it alone. I will not be afraid to relate to others; my peace cannot be stolen by recognizing a friend's anguish. Lord of compassion, may I reflect you in how I love and relate to everyone in my life. Fill me and don't stop meeting me in the realities of my life.

*What does it cost you to relate to others
without trying to fix them?*

As It Should Be

If we know he hears us every time we ask him,
we know we have what we ask from him.

1 JOHN 5:15 NCV

Ever-present One, you hear every request that comes your way. Your capacity is amazing. You don't grow weary responding to your children. Hear me today, Lord. I lay out my heart before you. I have confidence that you listen and respond. Give me eyes to see the answers to my prayers; it's likely that I'll forget I ever asked if you don't bring it to my attention. Encourage my soul today with the faithfulness of your grace that meets me. You are better than I can rightly know, but I want to see you more clearly as you are.

Thank you for your goodness, Lord, that follows me all the days of my life. What an extraordinary gift to be called your child and heir. I face today knowing that you are not only by my side but acting as my advocate and faithful provider. You are the best thing I've got in life. I'm so thankful for your constant companionship.

Do you believe that God provides all that you need?

Living on Camera

Whoever walks in integrity walks securely,
but he who makes his ways crooked will be found out.

PROVERBS 10:9 ESV

Holy God, my every thought is seen by you; I cannot keep my life hidden from your sight. Knowing this, may I stay on the path of righteousness, walking in sincerity and purity of heart all the days of my life. Today, I will be honest with myself and with others, letting my yes be yes and my no be no. When I am tempted to take the easy way out or to compromise my character in favor of my own comfort, remind me what the path of love looks like.

I submit my way to you again, Lord, knowing your wisdom will guide me into all truth. I don't need to be afraid of being found out if I'm living with a sincere heart that is set on you. I live in the security of being fully known and fully accepted just as I am. I'm not trying to be anyone else.

Are you living to please God or to please yourself?

Glorified Me

I know that I have not yet reached that goal,
but there is one thing I always do.
Forgetting the past and straining toward what is ahead.

PHILIPPIANS 3:13 NCV

God of glory, you are with me in the here and now. As I live with my eyes set on what's to come, let me be submitted to your grace that empowers me to shake off the mistakes of the past. I know that limitations are not permanent; keep me growing in you as I run the race of this life, looking to the prize at the end. Give me vision for the long-haul, that I wouldn't get sidetracked by minor problems that will work themselves out as I keep moving forward. Give me the wisdom I need to know when to rest and when to press on.

Whatever the future may bring, I believe it is better than what I can imagine asking. Giver of good gifts, I fix my eyes on you; you are the goal. I am running toward your goodness even as it meets me where I am.

What has been keeping you from moving forward in faith?

Father of Goodness

Praise the LORD in song,
for He has done excellent things;
Let this be known throughout the earth.

ISAIAH 12:5 NASB

Good Father, all you do is done with the stamp of your incredible love imprinted on it. I can't help but be amazed by the ways you have faithfully shown me that you are with me. There is nothing dictating that you pour out your love on me; you do it out of the overflow of your very being. It is too wonderful for me to understand. My mind cannot reason this kind of love. I am so grateful that you don't change based on my own moods or circumstances.

You are rock steady, never second-guessing your output. If I were to thank you every moment of every day of my life, it would not be enough to adequately equal the measure of your abundant goodness. But that's not what you're looking for, anyway. You love because it is who you are. Fill me up, Lord, that the overflow from my life will look like your character.

Where do you see the goodness of God in your life?

Life Gets Busy

The Lord answered her, "Martha, my beloved Martha.
Why are you upset and troubled, pulled away by all
these many distractions? Are they really that important?
Mary has discovered the one thing most important by
choosing to sit at my feet. She is undistracted, and I
won't take this privilege from her."

LUKE 10:41–42 TPT

Lord, when I am overwhelmed by all the tasks that need to
get done, would you gently remind me that your presence
is near, beckoning me? There are so many distractions that
pull at my attention every day, but peace is found in resting
at your feet. Give me an undivided heart that is fixed on
you. I offer you my attention right here in this moment. As
I quiet my heart and mind before you, I know that I will find
the wisdom I need. I won't be troubled by my to-do list
when I get back to work because your peace fills me with
the confidence and clarity I need.

In the busyness of life help me to intentionally practice
resting in you in stolen moments. As I practice your
presence throughout my day, I know that I will be better for
it—undistracted and filled with the light of your wisdom.

*How can you practice sitting in the presence of God
in the middle of a busy day?*

With you

We can confidently say,
"The LORD is my helper;
I will not fear;
what can man do to me?"

HEBREWS 13:6 ESV

God my help, you are the one I call upon in my hour of need. When I am faced with impossible situations that I have no idea how to navigate, I won't be afraid. I will run to you. You are God, my constant support and aid. Though people may try to ruin my reputation, they cannot take away the integrity of my heart. I will rest in you as my advocate and defender. I could be beaten down, dragged out, and still you would be my confidence. I put all my trust in you, fastening the hopes of my heart to the faithfulness of your character.

You do not fail, Lord. I will say it over again until it sinks into my consciousness: you do not fail! You are the victorious one, and nothing can stand in your way when you move. With you, I can face anything.

What do you need God's help with today?

In the Fight

The godly may trip seven times,
but they will get up again.
But one disaster is enough to overthrow the wicked.

PROVERBS 24:16 NLT

Mighty God, you are the sustainer of every living thing. I have partnered my life with yours; you have every right to my heart. I ask that you keep me close to you in the struggles of day-to-day life. I am not so foolish as to believe that the mundane doesn't matter. When I trip up, I need your help to get back up. You don't leave me when I need you. I know you aren't going to desert me when I call out for help. Thank you for your faithful love that keeps me close and safe. You never give up on me, and I won't give up on you.

Today, as I grab hold of the grace you so willingly give, would you make space for your miracles to happen? I know nothing is impossible with you. I trust you, and I eagerly await the ways you will show up as I look for you.

What keeps you getting up when you fall?

Absent of Judgment

"Do not judge, and you will not be judged;
do not condemn, and you will not be condemned.
Forgive, and you will be forgiven."

LUKE 6:37 NRSV

Gracious God, you withhold judgment when you could freely put every person in their place. Jesus, may I take your lead and extend forgiveness instead of judgment, may I give grace and mercy instead of a hot-headed lecture. Knowing that you are full of kindness to all, help me to be like you; you continually call people up and out of their shame and into the light of who they're meant to be.

When I am tempted to condemn someone based on their actions, would you give me eyes to see their humanity, the brokenness and heartache that they have endured. No one is immune to the struggles of life that either refine or harden us. I will extend forgiveness, knowing that I long for the same when I hastily hurt others. My heart will choose compassion instead of the cold-shoulder. Let me be a reflection of your better way, Lord.

Are you quick to judge those who offend you?

Honored

If anyone does not provide for his own, and especially
for those of his household, he has denied the faith
and is worse than an unbeliever.

1 TIMOTHY 5:8 NASB

God over all, nothing escapes your sight; nothing is hidden
from you. Even those who make deals in secret are seen by
you. You take care of those who are yours, and you expect
the same for those who follow you. May my life line up with
the values of your kingdom; otherwise, my faith is only a
claim. It doesn't mean anything if I speak words without
action to back them up. You honor those who uphold your
law of love. If it is not practiced in the home, it isn't worth
much out in the streets.

Lord, may I be consistent in the ways I serve you both at
home and outside of it. You see everything that I would like
you to overlook, but that's not how you work. Lord, give
me the grace to live with integrity and honor all for your
glory and for the benefit of those I love.

*How do you honor the Lord
with your family or close friends?*

Striving

"My presence will go with you, and I will give you rest."

EXODUS 33:14 ESV

Holy One, you are the longing of every weary heart. I'm tired of relying on my own strength to get by. It's exhausting. I don't have much more to give. My job and my family are suffering because I am nearing burnout. Lord, I know there must be a better way. Teach me to lean on your presence that provides me with the rest I need. There is no better way than depending on you.

God, you know how I tend to try things on my own until I run out of steam. I'd rather partner with you from the beginning and be renewed in your presence as I go. Your way is better, and I want to walk in it. I'm done with striving.

What can you stop working so hard at on your own?

Lesser Things

Let what you heard from the beginning abide in you.
If what you heard from the beginning abides in you,
then you will abide in the Son and in the Father.

1 JOHN 2:24 NRSV

Lord, my life is submitted to yours. As I abide in your goodness, I eat the fruit of your kingdom. Your kindness leads me to the truth of who you are You are so incredibly good, Father! May my life be so embedded in yours that anything that stands against your character would be clear to me. I want to spend my life on the things that matter.

Help me to be aligned with your compassion, Lord, as a vessel of your kindness to everyone I come into contact with. May my family know your love for them because of the way I treat them; may my friends see how generous you are in the reflection of my own generosity toward them. I know that if I write the law of your loyal love on my heart, it will be evident in my life as I choose your ways every day.

What kingdom values are evident in your life?

Better than Winning

When you do things, do not let selfishness or pride be your guide. Instead, be humble and give more honor to others than to yourselves.

PHILIPPIANS 2:3 NCV

Humble God, your instructions for a good life are so different than the world's advice. Instead of letting my own interests and pride guide me, you instruct that honoring others above myself is the way to live. I trust your wisdom; you know what you're doing. Lord, when I'm caught up in my own way making plans for my future, keep me soft in your love that leads me back to your side. If faced with a choice of honoring someone else or holding onto something I feel the right to have, may I choose honor.

Jesus, you built margin into your life, but you didn't serve your own whims or desires. I want to learn the same—to live like you did. Jesus, humble king, the example of your life is a beautiful, though difficult, model to follow. With your love filling and strengthening me, I can do even the hardest things.

Is honoring someone else over your own agenda worth it to you?

Increase My Faith

The apostles said to the Lord, "Increase our faith."

LUKE 17:5 NLT

Mighty God, you speak and the earth trembles. When you move, all of creation bows to your intentions. There is not a living thing that is outside of your grasp; you can easily reach anyone who cries out to you for help. You are the originator of all things including my own faith. Lord, as I live for you in this life, would you fill it with the goodness of your character? As your child, I know I can come to you with anything and you will receive me. And yet, even the apostles who journeyed with Jesus day-to-day asked for him to increase their faith. How much more do I need an increase?

Lord, I believe in you. The pattern of your love is all over my life. Even so, increase my faith, Lord, that as I journey with you, I would walk in greater confidence in who you are in me and I in you.

What do you need more faith for?

Unmerited Favor

Remember this: sin will not conquer you, for God already has! You are not governed by law but governed by the reign of the grace of God.

ROMANS 6:14 TPT

Great God, you have conquered me with your grace. Sin cannot control me because I have been overcome by you. With your great love covering my life all other powers and influences shrink. Lord, when I am battling fearful thoughts and jumping to conclusions fueled by anxiety, release your peace over my mind. Fear is not my leader, nor will it be! Your grace is what governs my life, and I won't be afraid of what may come.

With you by my side, I have nothing to fear. Lord, lead me in your great mercy that covers every weakness. Sin cannot have a hold on something that is covered by your power. May I remember this when the enemy tries to convince me otherwise. You are the wisest guide I've ever known; I will gladly follow you all the days of my life. Be glorified in me.

What has the most power over your thought life?

You Stay

All my longings lie open before you, LORD;
my sighing is not hidden from you.

PSALM 38:9 NIV

Comforter, you are the best friend I've ever known. You've been with me through it all: through the fiercest storms of my life and the greatest victories. There is no one I trust more than you, and yet I doubt even you at times who has never proven unworthy. I know that it is a reflection of my own brokenness and not yours.

Lord, you faithfully stay with me. You never give the silent treatment or punish me by pulling away your presence. You sit with me, patient and loving. When I'm angry, you hear me out. When I'm heartbroken, you move in close, holding me together. When I'm full of joy, you celebrate with me. When I'm goofy, you laugh with me. No matter what, Lord, you are there. You are so reliable. I will not stop sharing the depths of my heart with you, for you have shown how trustworthy you are.

Is there anything you've been hiding from the Lord?

Lessen My Grip

Do not forget to do good and to share,
for with such sacrifices God is well pleased.

HEBREWS 13:16 NKJV

Lord of all, you hold the key to the storehouse of heaven. Every resource ever possibly needed is found in your kingdom. You've got it all! As I live my life, may I not be tight-gripped with what I have. You are so generous, I want be generous too. And not just with money. May I loosen the grip of control over my time, leaving space to share it with others who would benefit. May I serve others when I have the chance, and if I don't have the chance, then I'm not looking hard enough.

Lord, you know my heart that just wants to stay in my comfortable existence, not doing much that stretches my boundaries. But I know that whatever I do, whether in the realm of my comfort or outside it, when I am doing good and sharing with others it is reflective of your ways. May I continue to follow in your footsteps.

How do you share the goodness of your life with others?

Unconditional Acceptance

"All that the Father gives Me will come to Me, and the one who comes to Me I will certainly not cast out."

JOHN 6:37 NASB

Merciful Father, you are so good in the way that you accept me with open arms. You did not have to, but you chose to. I cannot begin to thank you for your mercy that takes me in just as I am time and time again. I never have to dress myself up or convince you that I'm worthy of your attention or love. You are the one teaching me how valuable I am; you've known it all along. How could I describe the depths of the gratitude I feel? You never cast out your children.

When I think of the story of the prodigal son and how he squandered his inheritance, and the joy the father expressed at his return home, I am overcome by the thought of such a parent! Your goodness goes far beyond my comprehension, and yet here I am living in it. Thank you for your complete and unconditional acceptance of who I am; you make me comfortable in my own skin. I love you so much!

Do you believe that every part of you is fully accepted by God?

Aim for Harmony

Let us aim for harmony in the church
and try to build each other up.

ROMANS 14:19 NLT

God of unity, you did not make us isolated beings, each living our own lives in separate lanes. You created us for community, for fellowship, and for family. We were never meant to live alone, being only accountable to ourselves. Lord, in the family of believers, it is so easy to get frustrated with those who think and do things differently than I would. Jesus, when you instructed your disciples, you didn't tell them that they should strive to be right and only surround themselves with people they agreed with. No, you set the standard of love as the mark. Quarrels are inevitable, but unity takes intentionality.

Lord, may I be a builder of people, seeking to encourage them not tear them down or dismiss them when I disagree. Let harmony be the hallmark of your church not division. You are worthy of our unity, Jesus, as we all come under your headship.

Is harmony or order more important in a church setting?

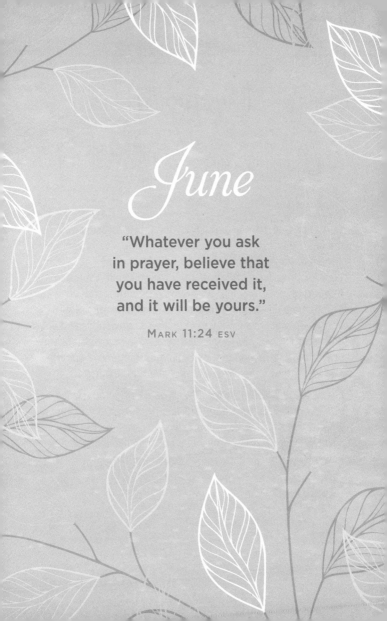

June

"Whatever you ask
in prayer, believe that
you have received it,
and it will be yours."

MARK 11:24 ESV

Dependable

Let not steadfast love and faithfulness forsake you;
bind them around your neck;
write them on the tablet of your heart.

PROVERBS 3:3 ESV

Constant One, I am grateful for your steady presence in my life. Whenever I need you, you are there. I've never known anyone as dependable as you. As I grow into your likeness, let faithfulness become an innate trait. As I depend on you, may I be an example of your steady love in my relationships with others. Let me not take for granted your ever-present help, just living life to please myself. I am blessed to know you, God; I ask for a fresh revelation of the power of your presence that turns mourning into dancing and water into wine. You always make things better!

I want to be like you, Lord, that I would bring your peace into chaotic situations and your love to anxiety-inducing circumstances. May your constant presence change me into the best version of myself, that I may live a life of faithful love right where you have planted me.

*Would your friends and family describe you
as being dependable?*

I Will Rejoice

This is the day the Lord has made;
We will rejoice and be glad in it.

PSALM 118:24 NKJV

Mighty God, I am grateful for another day to live and love! Thank you for giving me this fresh opportunity to know you and be known by you. I invite you into every area of my day; I long to see you reach into the details of it and bring the restoration and power of life that only you can. Let my heart overflow with gratitude and joy as I see you answering the prayers of my heart. There are no small asks to you, and nothing is too big for you to handle. I will rest in knowing that I don't have to face anything on my own.

With you, I know that all things are possible. Would you quiet the doubts of my mind with the power of your faithfulness in my life? I can't help but pour out my heart to you, God, for you are my joy and my living hope.

What can you rejoice in today?

With All

> "'Love the LORD your God with all your heart, all your
> soul, all your strength, and all your mind.' Also, 'Love
> your neighbor as you love yourself.'"
>
> LUKE 10:27 NCV

Lord over everything, in you I find fulfillment for every
longing. There is no desire that cannot be satisfied in
you; even as I pray that, my mind begins to rebel. But I do
believe that it is true—all of my hopes are quenched in you.
I don't need to rack up points with you by keeping track of
all my good deeds; I don't need to convince you that I'm
worthy because you are the one who made that possible.
It is in you that I find the life that I have been searching
for. What do I have to offer? That which no one else can
dictate or demand, and no one can take away.

Lord, today, and every day, I offer you my love with all
my heart, soul, strength, and mind. As I have been so
lavishly loved to life, I will love others in the same way I
love myself, preferring them as I would my own desires.
Let me give space for grace and mercy to fill in the cracks
of weaknesses, covering others with the same measure I
receive. Increase this capacity, Lord, as I grow in your love.

Are any parts of you holding back from loving God?

Every Moment

Teach us to number our days,
that we may gain a heart of wisdom.

PSALM 90:12 NIV

God of my days, come and fill me with the knowledge of
your heart in a new way. I invite you into my mind right
now; breathe your peace that brings calm to the rush of
thoughts going in multiple directions. I center myself in
your love. Let my soul be grounded in your truth, causing
all fear and anxiety to quiet and leave.

Today I remember that my days on this earth are limited.
Give me perspective that brings wisdom and not worry.
I trust that you know my moments as well as the larger
arc of the story. May my life be one lived with intention:
intentional love, the wisdom of seeing past my own
timeframe, and the purpose of sowing your kingdom
into others. I submit myself to the guidance of your Spirit
that leads me into the abundance of life, knowing every
moment matters.

Are you living with eternity's values in view?

All Grace

After you suffer for a short time, God, who gives all grace, will make everything right. He will make you strong and support you and keep you from falling. He called you to share in his glory in Christ, a glory that will continue forever.

1 PETER 5:10 NCV

God of grace, you are the restorer of every broken thing. There is nothing beyond your ability to heal or make right. Keeper of my heart, you offer the strength I don't have on my own to face the giants in my life. You are a strong support and the firmest foundation. Every trial and every heartbreaking season is only temporary; it won't last forever. Keep my eyes fixed on you, the one who called me in the first place. Then I won't be lost in the dense fog of disillusion.

Let your light burn off the haze that hides you, and as it shines I will find that your glory is brighter than the sunniest days of my youth. You are the goodness that carries me through every storm and trial into a place of renewal. In the light, I see that nothing has been wasted. Master Restorer, you bring life to everything you touch.

Where do you need God's grace to keep you from falling?

Humble Help

If another believer is overcome by some sin, you who
are godly should gently and humbly help that person
back onto the right path. And be careful not to fall into
the same temptation yourself.

GALATIANS 6:1 NLT

Jehovah, your ever-present help keeps me from falling
into the dark ravines of sin and shame. Even when I do
stumble, you keep bringing me back to the path of life
where your light shines. When I see my brother or sister
caught in sin that leads them to shame spirals, may I be a
voice of compassion and gentleness that calls them back
to the light, reminding them of the truth of who they are
in you. Let love be the support that carries them out of
the entanglement of sin. Let me be a humble voice that
reminds them of the freedom you have already given them.

Spirit of truth, keep me secure in your affectionate wisdom
that I would not fall into the same trap. Thank you for your
persistent grace as a reminder that no one is lost or too far
gone. Good God, may your people be brought back into
your light to walk in the way of love and truth.

*How do you approach those who are living
under the weight of sin?*

Before Confessing

If we confess our sins, he who is faithful and just will
forgive us our sins and cleanse us
from all unrighteousness.

1 JOHN 1:9 NRSV

Merciful Father, thank you for your faithful forgiveness that
covers every act done out of the lack of love in my life. You
are grace-giver, and I come to you today with my hands
open to receive all that you have to give. Lord, right now I
confess the sins that I've been participating in. Every failing
that goes against your kingdom's values: every act of
jealousy, dishonor, selfishness, and lust.

Lord, thank you for your remarkable love that covers every
wrong motivation in my life. No one else offers the sort of
mercy that I find in you. How great you are, God! May it
fuel me with grace and humility to love those who seem
unlovable, for I know at my worst, still you love me. As I
soak in the acceptance you freely bestow, may I become
more confident in your strong love to save and restore.

Are you willing to forgive those who have wronged you?

We Are Family

I bow my knees before the Father, from whom every
family in heaven and on earth is named.

EPHESIANS 3:14–15 ESV

Perfect Father, in you I find the parent I never knew I
needed. You are better than my mother or my father, and I
am faithfully found secure in the love that you freely offer.
I am so grateful that you do not make individuals to act
independently of each other. You have set us in families,
and every person on earth is your descendant. When I am
quick to judge others as strange or undesirable, would
you fill me with the compassion of a family member? The
kind of compassion that loves even those whom I don't
understand or prefer.

I humble myself before you, Father; teach me your ways of
kindness that draw people in rather than push them out. I
submit myself to you, wanting to know you in the context
of brothers and sisters who receive the same love, care,
and affection from you, the perfect parent. Thank you for
the reminder that we are all made in your image with no
exceptions.

*Do you treat others with the same respect or compassion
you would a family member?*

My Deepest Pain

"Blessed are those who mourn,
for they shall be comforted."

MATTHEW 5:4 NASB

God of comfort, meet me in the middle of my deepest pain. My bleeding heart needs your healing touch. You don't ask that I be okay in order to mend. You don't expect me to clean myself up before you are willing to come sit with me. Your peaceful presence meets me in my mess, in the dirt where I can't even lift my tear-stained cheeks to see who it is that holds me. You don't push me into a race when my legs won't hold the weight of me. No, when I cannot stand, you carry me to a place of rest. You give space to my pain, validating the weight of my grief. Thank you for your patient presence that heals my broken heart.

In you I find the strength I need for every day. And in you I relish the comfort of knowing you understand the depths of the pain of my experience. I don't have to explain myself to you. I trust that you will lead me through my grief with your healing power. Hold on to me, Lord, when my grip is weak.

In your deepest pain, have you known the comfort of God's presence?

Pay It Forward

Remember that judgment is merciless for the one who judges others without mercy. So by showing mercy you take dominion over judgment!

JAMES 2:13 TPT

Gracious God, only you have all the knowledge and power to judge rightly. When I am tempted to judge others based on their careless actions or thoughtless words, remind me of the mercy I have been shown. Your Word says that mercy is better than judgment; may I remember this in the nitty-gritty of the frustrations and tensions that happen in the day-to-day. For those who repeatedly offend and wound me, may I have the grace to extend mercy along with wisdom to set boundaries.

You are good. You don't demand that we stay in abusive relationships, but you do set the bar for how we handle our own hearts toward others. May every thought of my heart be drenched in your mercy, leading me to compassion for those who are challenging. Thank you, God, that I can rely on your help. I don't have to do this on my own.

When dealing with difficult people, are you quick to judge and dismiss them?

Security

"Behold, I will bring to it health and healing,
and I will heal them and reveal
to them abundance of prosperity and security."

JEREMIAH 33:6 ESV

Lord, you are my firm foundation. You are the rock that I stand upon, and you are immovable. You are the security that my heart longs for in an ever-changing world. Thank you, God, that you remain the same in every season; reveal the abundance of your kingdom in my life. I know that in you is more than enough peace and love to go around for all eternity. Let your goodness, kindness, and generosity be evident in the way I live.

I rely on you to produce the fruit of your Spirit in my life. My healing is found in you; I will be made whole. May your joy fill my heart as I devote myself to you. Hem me in and keep me safely surrounded by your perfect love that drives out every one of my fears. You are the one I trust. There is no one else like you.

Where do you feel safest in your life?

For your Glory

"Seek first His kingdom and His righteousness,
and all these things will be added to you."

MATTHEW 6:33 NASB

King of Kings, you are the one I seek above all else. To be like you is the goal of my life; I know that your ways are better than the most benevolent ruler on earth. I lay down every ambition to be great for my own sake. I don't want to live with a shortsighted view. Your kingdom's values don't get stale or outdated. They stand the test of time. Why would I waste my life trying to get the next best thing? Your steadfast love is the string that runs through every generation.

Spirit of God, guide me into the way of blamelessness that is found only on your pathway of peace. Let my heart be set on your will and intentions, knowing that there is none better. When I see others gaining ground in their goals and dreams, let me be reminded that life is not about competition. When I follow you, I will find the life I am looking for. In you every aspiration is fulfilled. Keep me from getting distracted. May my eyes remain locked on you.

What are the motivations of the plans you make?

Reason for Success

The LORD will be your confidence,
And will keep your foot from being caught.

PROVERBS 3:26 NASB

God, I come to you with all my dreams and goals laid out before you. As I follow you, your goodness finds me. What a privilege to be walking in the light of your favor. You know how easily I rely on my own abilities to get things done. When my strength is depleted, and I have nothing else to give, when there is still much to do and many needs left unmet, I fall into you. I was never meant to be the one to do it all.

You alone are able to meet every need. It is not my job. Whether I fail or succeed, I am confident that you are big enough to cover it all. My confidence is not found in my own ability. Help me when I edge toward perfectionism. In you is where everyone and everything finds their satisfaction. Thank you, Lord.

Do you have more confidence in your abilities or in God's?

My Parachute

When I am afraid,
I will put my trust in you.

PSALM 56:3 NLT

Prince of Peace, I am grateful for your presence that is always with me. Your love follows me even when I think I've lost my way. There is nowhere I can go where you are not. You are all around me. Spirit of God, come and cover me now with your grace. You see my fears; you know what I'm hesitantly skirting around these days. Keep my heart secure in you. I put my trust in you. Where uncertainty causes me to pull into myself, I purposefully lay it all out before you.

Here are my concerns, God, I give you full access to them. I don't want to hold back from you when I know that you are able to lead me with perfect peace. I trust you to guard my heart in your love. Right now, I receive your gentle instruction. I am holding onto you.

What do you do with fear when it overtakes you?

Bloom

Grow in the grace and knowledge of our Lord and Savior Jesus Christ. To him be glory both now and forever! Amen.

2 PETER 3:18 NIV

Lord my God, you are the source of life. I am connected to you, Father, through Jesus. I know that whatever fruit my life produces is based on the health of my root system. With my roots planted by streams of living water, they grow deep in the knowledge of you. As I grow in grace and the goodness of your person, the fruit of my life reveals that you are working in and through me. Every good thing in my life is a result of your constant presence feeding and pruning my character.

Let the fruit of my life reveal the sweetness of your kingdom—fruit that nourishes the hungry and satisfies the curious. You are nothing if not good. As I grow in the light of your kindness, may my life come into full bloom for your glory. All the days of my life are yours, God. Have your way!

Do you see the fruit of God's kingdom at work in your life as you grow in him?

Thoughts Captured

Think about the things that are good and worthy
of praise. Think about the things that are true
and honorable and right and pure and beautiful
and respected.

PHILIPPIANS 4:8 NCV

Lord, as I live surrendered to you, fill my life with the
evidence of your presence. When my mind starts to
wander down alleys of worry filling my thoughts with
confusion, call me back to your pathway of peace where
all things are made clear in the light. As I meditate on your
Word, I am training to think about those things that are
good and pure; life will flow into my thought life as I set my
mind on the values of your kingdom. When I consider your
impeccable character, I cannot help but praise you.

I honor you, Lord, and your goodness that shines from
everything you do. Everything that you touch has the
mark of love that brings life. How could I worry when your
indicators are all over my life? Thank you, Lord. I adore the
way you make all things right in you.

*Do you pay attention to where your thoughts go
throughout the day?*

Choose Your Way

A man without self-control
is like a city broken into and left without walls.

PROVERBS 25:28 ESV

Holy One, you set the standard of excellence, showing us the best way to live. I am grateful that even in the mysteries of your ways you pave a clear path for us to follow. We are not slaves to our own desires or to our perceptions. We were set free in order to freely choose you and your ways. Today I get to practice self-control that puts up boundaries for my own protection and health. As I choose when to speak and when not to, when to act and when to sit back, I ask that you offer your wisdom that always knows best.

Thank you that there is grace in the choosing. I am not a slave to my preferences and you are not limited by my choices. What freedom there is in you. I am so grateful for the example of Jesus' choices that illustrate the power of margin. We were never meant to be accessible to everyone at all times. Jesus, teach me to have value in placing limits where and when they need to be established. Cover all my choices with grace as I follow you.

Do you actively put up healthy boundaries in your life?

Good Sense

Those with good sense are slow to anger,
and it is their glory to overlook an offense.

PROVERBS 19:11 NRSV

Merciful God, I want to reflect your character. It is in my nature to react to offense with frustration, if not full-on ire. You, who have every reason to be angry, are slow to become upset. Teach me, in your goodness and patience, to overlook offenses that don't matter. What relief there is in letting those things go. Where there is indignation may I test my own heart, seeking out the cause of the innate response.

I don't want to be consistently reactive. Instead, may my heart be full of good sense to separate offense from wickedness. I don't want to live as a victim to others' moods or poor choices. As I submit myself to you, God, I bind my heart to yours. Your heart is full of kindness and mercy; as I walk in your way of love, I find that it covers a multitude of wrongdoings. Thank you for your better method.

Are you quick to anger?

Contentment

Each of you should continue to live in whatever
situation the Lord has placed you,
and remain as you were when God first called you.

1 CORINTHIANS 7:17 NLT

Faithful One, you are so consistent in your love toward me. When I think over the journey that my walk with you has looked like, I see how your faithfulness has followed me every step. I believe that you are working for my benefit, even in the areas that look barren and dry. May my heart find its contentment in knowing you, whatever circumstances I find myself in. I trust that you are my perfect portion.

When I am tempted to run away from the realities of life, meet me with the power of your grace to remain faithfully present. May I stay rooted and grounded in the strength of your love, trusting that you offer everything I need right when I need it. I will not be found lacking, for in you is every possible tool I could ever require. May my heart find its satisfaction in you, my faithful friend.

Where does your contentment come from?

Ultimate Guide

I want you to pattern your lives after me,
just as I pattern mine after Christ.

1 CORINTHIANS 11:1 TPT

Everlasting God, you are the best leader. I submit my life to you, trusting you to guide me in truth with your constant presence as my companion. I will live my life looking to the example of Jesus. Let courageous compassion be the hallmark of my relationships. May kindness flow from my words and actions, calling attention to your faithful love. When I speak, may my words be delivered in grace-covered truth.

As I work, let the product be faithfully reflective of both your creativity and stability. With your life as the prime model, Jesus, I will never go wrong by choosing to act in lovingkindness toward those who are commonly overlooked. When I am tempted to choose my own comfort over obedience to you, remind me of your persistent pursuit of my own heart. Help me to courageously push past fear and live as you would in submission to the will of the Father.

What leads you in life?

Nothing to Condemn

There is now no condemnation
for those who are in Christ Jesus.

ROMANS 8:1 NASB

Lord of my freedom, you have covered my every weakness
and failure with your incredible love. There is nothing in
my submitted life outside of your grace. Nothing is out of
bounds; you reach every part. God of abundance, you don't
lack in mercy. You are a waterfall of unending kindness
flowing over your people. Your love brings the relief my
weighed-down soul longs for.

God, may I daily remember that there is no condemnation
for me because I am yours. You withhold judgment and
instead release your mercy over my life. How could I
begin to thank you? I will walk in the confidence of your
forgiveness, not beating myself up for mistakes I make along
the way. You have saved me from a life of guilt and shame. It
wasn't my own good intentions or thoughtful deeds that got
me out of that mess. Thank you for a clean slate.

*When you make mistakes, do you feel the weight of
condemnation or the relief of God's covering grace?*

Never Too Much

"You don't have enough faith," Jesus told them. "I tell you the truth, if you had faith even as small as a mustard seed, you could say to this mountain, 'Move from here to there,' and it would move. Nothing would be impossible."

MATTHEW 17:20 NLT

Great God, there is no situation too big for you to handle. When I look in your Word, it is full of examples of people who had confidence that you would come through for them time and again. Jesus, you yourself said that if we have faith even as small as a tiny mustard seed, we could command a mountain to move and it would.

I want faith like that. With your power as my barometer, I can say, "Peace, be still" to a raging storm and it will calm. I pray that as I walk in your ways, I will have the assurance of you coming through when I step out—all for your glory. You are the God who makes the impossible possible. What a glorious mystery. I don't want to simply marvel at this, I want to walk in it. Increase my faith even as I step out.

What impossible situation is waiting for you to step out in faith?

Selflessness

Let each of you look out not only for his own interests, but also for the interests of others.

PHILIPPIANS 2:4 NKJV

God of compassion, thank you for your affection that goes beyond any boundaries that we set. Your limitless love goes further than the farthest reaches of the galaxy. Your endless supply is always accessible. Taking my cues from you, I look to those in front of me, considering their interests as well as my own. I don't want to be small-minded in the way I live my life; may I live with intentionality, giving away kindness like it's going out of style... except it never will!

When my vision gets narrow and I can only see my little section of the world, I pray for eyes to view the bigger picture: to really see the people around me. In a world full of self-centeredness, may I live considerately with unity as the goal. Thank you, Lord, that I was made to operate in a family and a community, working with others.

How can you practice selflessness today?

Make You Proud

Do your best to present yourself to God as one
approved by him, a worker who has no need to be
ashamed, rightly explaining the word of truth.

2 TIMOTHY 2:15 NRSV

Father, as your image-bearer, I want to make you proud of
how I represent you in my life. With truth guiding my mind
and your faithful love as my motivation, I offer all I am to
serve your purposes on the earth. May your kingdom be
made real in my life, so everyone who knows me sees that
your goodness is real and it is accessible to all. Thank you
for filling my life with your mercy and grace, so I am able to
partner with you in extending compassionate kindness to
others. Let me be diligent in exhibiting your character and
sharing your heart with those around me.

I ask for boldness to reveal the meaning of my own life
with those who are unfamiliar with your ways. There is
no one like you, perfect Father, and I want all the world
to know the transformation you bring. You are a master
restorer, melting hearts of stone and loving the dead to life.

What in others makes you proud to know them?

Take Courage

"Have I not commanded you? Be strong and of good courage; do not be afraid, nor be dismayed, for the Lord your God is with you wherever you go."

JOSHUA 1:9 NKJV

Ever-present One, you are a true companion and help, always with me in times of trouble as well as rest. When fear tries to bully me, I will remember that I am not alone. When disappointment approaches my door, I will remind myself that you are with me no matter the circumstance. You know my heart is tempted to follow the pathway of dismay, but your love is better. Thank you for the choice that is freely mine to decide which energy I will partner with: courage or fear.

I know that you have given me grace to empower me to stand in confidence even when logic screams to run away. I will not live my life deferring to fear's intimidation tactics. Today I choose to be brave, for I know that you are with me. I will walk in the way of courage with your love as my firm foundation. I find all the resolve I need in the strength of your support.

What do you need courage to face today?

Forgive Me

Consider my affliction and my trouble,
and forgive all my sins.

PSALM 25:18 ESV

God of mercy, you cover me in your great love, forgiving all my sin. When I was overwhelmed by the weight of shame, you lifted my guilt that allowed me to follow after you with the grace of one who has been set free! Lord, there is no limit to the mercy you extend. There is nothing I do that is beyond the grip of your grace. Instead of running from you, may I come to you with every failure, knowing you won't turn me away.

I cannot adequately thank you for the ways in which you continually save me from myself. You are incredible in the countless ways you pour out your love over my life. I could never deserve the favor you give. Even in my trouble, you have set me free to dance upon the discontent of my failure. Thank you for your faithfulness.

Do you believe that when you ask for it,
you receive full forgiveness?

New Heart

"He who believes in Me, as the Scripture has said,
out of his heart will flow rivers of living water."

JOHN 7:38 NKJV

Infinite One, you are the source of living water. Your
refreshing fountain of life revives even the most destitute
soul. Thank you for freely flowing in and through me—what
a wonderful gift! Not only am I brought to life in you, but
this same power gushes out of me. King of kings, you are
the originator of all the greatness we see, and yet you
are so much better. May I not hoard the life in my heart,
causing the water to grow stale.

Lord, I know that your kingdom is ever-increasing; may
I freely offer all that you have given, not keeping the
restorative life you have given a secret. As I live my life
generously, I trust that you will continue to pour out your
lifegiving love over me. In you, my heart has come alive.
Thank you for making me new. I offer you all the praise I
have. You are so worthy.

What is flowing from your heart lately?

By Your Grace

"If you forgive those who sin against you, your heavenly Father will forgive you. But if you refuse to forgive others, your Father will not forgive your sins."

MATTHEW 6:14–15 NLT

Gracious God, you are so generous in your mercy to all. I cannot presume to be like you yet refuse to forgive. With some people, it is easier to forgive them than not. The deeper the wound inflicted by the person, the harder it is to pardon them. When I'm finding it hard to let go of the rights, I feel over the pain that someone inflicted, give me the grace I need to trust that you are the only one who has the right to withhold forgiveness. And yet, you don't! Keep my heart set on you, so even in this struggle I go deeper into your heart of love.

Your compassion covers a multitude of sins; I will look to your kindness and not theirs, Lord, when I need the gentle push in the right direction. May I not hold others to a standard I would not submit to myself. Cover me with your considerate love.

Who do you need grace to forgive?

How Much

"The very hairs of your head are all numbered."

MATTHEW 10:30 NKJV

Creator, you have every detail of my life recorded. You know the number of freckles on my face, the hairs on my head, and you know the deepest hopes of my heart. There is nothing about me that is a mystery to you. I am grateful to know that the one who knows me the best loves me the most. Lord, give me a new revelation of the depths of care you have, sending any doubts I have packing. When I am caught up in the stress of the unknown, help me take rest in the awareness that you see and know all.

As I yield my heart to you again, fill me with the conviction of your understanding; you are for me, and I can trust you to guide me. I welcome you to invade my life with your perfect peace that brings the clarity I need. I am yours.

Does God's intimate knowledge of you bring you comfort?

Joyful Surrender

"All authority in heaven and on earth
has been given to me."

MATTHEW 28:18 NIV

Holy Father, you are the maker of all things. There is nothing that doesn't fall under your influence; your authority trumps every other in this world. I gladly surrender to you, knowing that you are not a power-hungry dictator. You rule rightly, and I can trust you to lead me with the light of your presence. Though your ways are different than the ways of this world, your methods are higher. With the law of love as the ultimate measure, I walk in the path of peace that you paved.

Jesus, you hold all authority, in both heaven and earth; living for you cannot be a poor choice. There is no better leader to serve, for you know every outcome to every situation, and you are the victorious one. Today, I joyfully give you all I am again. You are benevolent and kind, and I am privileged to be yours.

What can you surrender to God today?

July

He will answer
the prayers of the needy;
he will not reject their prayers.

Psalm 102:17 ncv

Deleting Criticism

Do not let any unwholesome talk
come out of your mouths,
but only what is helpful for building others up
according to their needs,
that it may benefit those who listen.

EPHESIANS 4:29 NIV

Wonderful Counselor, your wisdom offers all the building blocks needed for life. You offer it freely to all who seek out your advice. Where I've been lax with my words, help me find the self-control I need to keep the words of my mouth life-giving. Your Word says there is the power of life and death in the tongue. Somehow, though I take other parts of your Word seriously, I consistently (or conveniently) skim past this.

Lord of my heart, I want my words to be a reflection of the love inside my heart not futile frustrations or negativity. Give me revelation of the power of the words I choose, that I would begin to weigh them wisely. Where criticism turns into cutting someone down, it can never be for their benefit or my own. May my mouth become a pure reflection of a pure heart that loves you.

*How often do you spend your time criticizing people
when talking about them?*

Your Reasons

Every man's way is right in his own eyes,
But the LORD weighs the hearts.

PROVERBS 21:2 NASB

God over all, you see directly into the intentions of my heart, measuring what others do not see. I have given my life to you; I walk with you purposefully. But still, how easy it is to get caught up in the day-to-day, forgetting to invite your input to weigh in on the attitudes behind my actions. Lord, would you enlighten me today with your love, letting me see clearly what is beneficial and what is not? I don't want to be stuck in a rut, explaining away why I do the things I do if they're not reflective of your character. In your goodness, I find who I want to become. May I not get stuck in who I've been, complacently trudging along in my own biases and off-kilter motives.

Lord, your love is like a tuning fork. As I soak in your presence, you bring what is out of balance back into alignment. Even now, I set my mind and heart on you. Fill me with your wisdom that gives purpose to the mundane and keeps me on the pathway of peace.

Do you ever stop to think about what the motivations of your heart are when you're on auto-pilot?

While I Wait

They desire a better, that is, a heavenly country.
Therefore God is not ashamed to be called their God,
for He has prepared a city for them.

HEBREWS 11:16 NKJV

Advocate, thank you for the hope that is found in you.
Every desire finds its fulfillment in you. When I look around
this earth searching for a society that lives with your values,
tearing down walls instead of building them, I cannot find
it. There is so much beauty to be found in every nation, and
yet none has got it all right. How I long for the day when
Jesus returns and sets all the wrong things right; when
neighbors will look out for each other with peace as their
best interest and not fear as their watch guard.

Lord, your kingdom is better than the most successful
nation on earth. I align myself to your heavenly way,
knowing that this place is not my true home. You are found
in the waiting, and you know what it is to practice patience.
In every area of delay in my life, keep my mind filled with
the clarity of peace and wisdom. May my eyes be fixed on
the coming goodness, grateful for the evidence that is with
us today.

How do you deal with having to wait for something?

I Am Free

"Then you will know the truth,
and the truth will make you free."

JOHN 8:32 NCV

Victorious One, you infuse my heart with the joy of one who once was limited but now is free. Jesus, you laid out the truth of the Father, leveling the playing field for every heart. The religious don't have an advantage, and the beggar doesn't have a disadvantage when it comes to knowing you. No one can buy your love or forgiveness; you freely give to all who ask. What a glorious reality that not only does the truth of God's extravagant love poured out set us free, it sets every person from every background free.

God, where I have become exclusive in my thinking, fooled into letting pride keep me from sharing your incredible life-changing love, may I be set free to share the truth of your Word with everyone. Thank you that liberty is not full of obligations; it sets me free to choose how I will live my life. I rejoice in the choices I get to make with and for you today. I am so grateful.

*Are there any areas that you feel bound
by obligation instead of freedom?*

Simplicity

I'm afraid that just as Eve was deceived by the serpent's clever lies, your thoughts may be corrupted and you may lose your single-hearted devotion and pure love for Christ.

2 CORINTHIANS 11:3 TPT

God of my heart, you are my first love—the greatest love—of my life. I am overcome when I consider your faithfulness to me even in my deliberate wandering. Where my heart has filled with the love of other things that compete for your attention and affection, I ask that you open my eyes to the greatness of who you are. I don't want to waste energy on lesser loves that have nothing lasting to give me. With the clarity of a sound mind, I consider the fruit of your presence in my life.

Your affections aren't dictated by my response. You don't hold back your friendship when I am distancing myself. You are so much better than anyone I've ever known. Why would I let my heart be divided when you are the endless goodness I've been searching for? Let the pull of distractions fade, as I reset my heart and mind on you.

What has distracted you from God's love lately?

A Season

For everything there is a season,
and a time for every matter under heaven:

ECCLESIASTES 3:1 NRSV

Lord over all, your timing is impeccable. Just when I think you have forgotten about a promise, you come through with your provision. Though waiting times differ, your faithfulness never diminishes. May I be in touch with the seasons of life. When I am in a barren winter season where I need to rest, I won't find the growth and lightness that spring brings. Keep my heart sensitive to you, so when the season doesn't match my hope, I see clearly from your perspective, knowing that time will come. Give me unwavering hope in your goodness to see you come through at every point in life.

I'm trying to not lose confidence, Lord, but in some areas the waiting has been long and the projection looks weak. Give me strength to hold onto your great expectation, even if mine dwindles a bit. I submit my heart to your timing, knowing you are trustworthy.

Do you sense what type of spiritual season you're in?

Not Defeated

Every child of God defeats this evil world,
and we achieve this victory through our faith.

1 JOHN 5:4 NLT

Great King, just when I thought I was down and out, when the walls of darkness had closed in and I thought they would crush me, you showed up with your strong hand of mercy to save me. I am not a victim to the world or its ways; I am not doomed to be stuck under another's thumb all the days of my life. I am free in you, Jesus. It's in that freedom I find my victory. As your child, my inheritance is bigger than my current circumstances.

When you shine your light on me, I can see, with eyes of faith, the better path you have laid out. I don't have to walk in the ways of this world that lead to death. I will walk with you on the pathway of peace. In choosing to walk in your example of love, I become an overcomer. Thank you, Father, for the different tactics you take that are unlike the world and its ways. Your standard is better.

*What areas of feeling defeated can you invite
the Lord into today?*

Willingly Tethered

Perfume and incense bring joy to the heart,
and the pleasantness of a friend
springs from their heartfelt advice.

PROVERBS 27:9 NIV

Faithful Friend, you are the best companion I've ever known. No one is like you. You are more faithful than my own family. You are willing to go where I go and meet me on my terms, and yet you are constantly pulling me out of my shell and into the great unknown where you love to venture. What a joy it is to know you and to be known by you. When I am too weak to leave my home, you keep me company. When I have problems that need solving, you listen with the ear of a skilled counselor; you offer the best advice I could ever hope to find.

With you, my closest confidant, I find I can just be myself; I don't have to put on airs or try to clean myself up. You delight in me just as I am, and I can't help but do the same. Thank you for your friendship that is more meaningful than any other relationship I've known. You are the one in whom my soul delights and finds its home.

What is it like when you are around your closest friends?

Whatever I Ask

> "If in my name you ask me for anything, I will do it."
>
> JOHN 14:14 NRSV

Good Father, you are the one in whom I find every longing of my heart filled. There is not a day that goes by when I don't ask you for something, yet I don't want to find myself constantly demanding what I do not yet have. I find my satisfaction in knowing you; everything else is a perk of relationship. I know that your provision is faithful in every season. I am not a beggar, and you are not stingy. When I ask for bread, you do not offer me a rock. When I am hungry, you don't present me with a bowl of sand.

You are a good father, taking care of your children. I am so grateful to be called one. Give me boldness to ask freely, and a humble heart that receives all you have to give with grace and joy. With confidence, I come to you today, my provider.

What have you held back from asking God?

Much Need

Even lions may get weak and hungry,
but those who look to the LORD
will have every good thing.

PSALM 34:10 NCV

Great God, you constantly pour out goodness from the overflow of your generous character. There is nothing that I could ever have need of that you could not supply. You offer strength to the weak, healing to the broken, and comfort to the brokenhearted. You build up those who have been torn down; you offer the help of a friend and advocate. You do not throw money at problems as some rich rulers do; you get down in the dirt and fix things with your own strong arms.

You have every resource at your disposal. My problems pale in comparison to the greatness of your means. I will not be afraid of ruin or of lack; it is not my own reliability I trust in. When my strength runs out, there you are with abundant grace. You freely offer help whenever I need it. I lean on you, everlasting God.

What do you need today?

Bearing Gifts

There are varieties of gifts, but the same Spirit. And
there are varieties of ministries, and the same Lord.
There are varieties of effects, but the same God who
works all things in all persons. But to each one is given
the manifestation of the Spirit for the common good.

1 CORINTHIANS 12:4–7 NASB

Wonderful One, you are the giver of all good things. You
pour out your gifts to all in differing measures and in
unique ways. I am thankful for the gifts you have deposited
in me. I know that I did not get left out when you were
deciding who gets what. Keep my heart from jealousy that
would see another's gifts as more valuable than my own.

Your love does not discriminate; let my confident
assurance in your character translate to confidence in who
you've created me to be. I don't want to be anyone else.
No, I want to come alive in who you have purposed me to
become. Let me never forget how you delight in me. As I
find my confidence in your Spirit that fills me, let me see
the beauty that you have put in others. I pray that I would
value those with gifts and temperaments different from my
own. You are Lord over all; you are the unifier!

*What gifts has God put in you to reflect
his character to others?*

Beloved Child

You are altogether beautiful, my love;
there is no flaw in you.

SONG OF SOLOMON 4:7 ESV

Loving Father, your incredible love welcomes me like a
bear hug; your warm presence is the most hospitable
atmosphere I've ever known. As a dearly loved child, I can
freely come and go as I please. That is almost too good to
be true. Thank you for your love that delights in me just as
I am. As I soak in your attention receiving the affection you
freely give, I feel joy bubbling over the brim of my heart.

You are extraordinary, Lord. I'm running out of words to
describe your goodness. You are the light that brings
warmth to every living thing; we grow in the brightness of
your great favor. Secure me in my identity as your child,
so I go out into the world and throw kindness around like
confetti, brightening the day of those who encounter it. Let
my confidence grow each day as I soak in the oil of your
love that draws out all impurities.

*What does it mean for you to know that
you are child of the King?*

Sadness

Cast all your anxiety on him,
because he cares for you.

1 PETER 5:7 NRSV

Gracious God, I come to you with my whole heart today. I don't want to hold anything back from you. Here are the worries that have been running around the track of my mind. They have worn me down, and I don't know what to do with them. Only you see the depth of feeling in my heart. Here is the sadness that has been lining my heart. Come and comfort me as only you can and bring relief. Let the healing salve of your presence take away the sting of grief.

I know that you care for me. God, bring life to the parts that I don't even know how to name. I will not stop turning to you because it's only in you that I find the reprieve my weighed-down soul longs for. Take my anxiety and remove it from me. Bring the rest that only you can, and I will live another day singing your praises. Who is like you, Lord?

What weighty emotions can you offer God today?

Beautiful Future

"No eye has seen, no ear has heard,
and no mind has imagined
what God has prepared
for those who love him."

1 CORINTHIANS 2:9 NLT

Almighty God, you see the end from the beginning and every space in between. Your eyes see every possible outcome. Why would I want to go it alone? You are my greatest treasure; I would not trade you for all the gold in the world. Your guidance is less like a tightrope and more like a river; I will not fear a misstep leading to a drastic fall. Rather, I will trust that I am being carried in the stream. Even when I get stuck in the rocks at the edges, all I need is a gentle push to get right back into the flow of where your river is taking me.

With your grace as my covering, I do not fear the future; I hold tightly to hope, believing that you have all the details worked out for my good. I am resting in your presence that carries me along. No dark night can keep me from the goodness that sunbreak brings. Thank you, Lord!

Do you feel hope or dread for the future?

A Voice

He will care for the needy and neglected
when they cry to him for help.
The humble and helpless will know his kindness,
for with a father's compassion he will save their souls.

PSALM 72:12-13 TPT

Compassionate Lord, you are an advocate for the voiceless. You not only see the neglected and needy in society, but you care for them. Your great kindness answers their cries for help. In your great compassion, you offer the wealth of your kingdom to their weary souls. Let me reflect your goodness in the way I live my life. If I ignore the poor and needy around me, surely, I am not living in your likeness. There are no second-class citizens in your kingdom. We are all sons and daughters on equal footing.

Lord, when I see my brother in need, move my heart with compassion. Let my life make space for those that the world would rather ignore. Let me live with thoughtful consideration for everyone I rub elbows with, for I know I will find you there. Let me lift my own voice with yours, calling out for justice and equality.

Who can you speak up for?

Obedience

I will keep on obeying your instructions
forever and ever.

PSALM 119:44 NLT

Good God, when I am breezily living in the freedom
you have blessed me with, may I not forget the benefit
of boundaries. I pray that my heart wouldn't grow cold
toward your instructions for life. Keep me malleable in
your hand. Spirit of God, may I remain sensitive to your
voice. Let me distinguish your instructions from those that
are man-made. Your Word is full of wisdom; when I am
following you, I know I will find renewal in obedience.

Thank you for your grace that is a constant flow, not a
sporadic drip. I don't need to hoard it now, afraid that one
day it will dry up. As I continue to submit my life to your
grace, let everything I do be done in response to your
character, not as a reaction or trigger to false beliefs. I
can trust that everything you ask of me is done with my
benefit, and the benefit of others, in mind. I yield to your
better way.

What has the Lord been nudging you toward?

My Strength

"Be strong and bold; have no fear or dread of them,
because it is the LORD your God who goes with you;
he will not fail you or forsake you."

DEUTERONOMY 31:6 NRSV

Mighty God, though my body's strength fails me, I know that the strength of your Spirit never does. When I am weary and tired of doing the right thing, fill me with your grace that empowers me to continue. With you on my side, I won't have to ever face anything alone. You infuse me with courage to stand strong with you; my confidence is in your larger-than-life presence.

The mountains must look like anthills from your vantage point, Lord. I can't help but laugh with joy. You have totally got this! I get to partner with you, and what an amazing honor that is. With boldness, I walk into the battle by your side. What enemy would take you on? In any case, I am not afraid because you are with me. What is there to dread when you are by my side?

What battle feels too large to face on your own?

God Bless You

"The LORD bless you and keep you;
the LORD make his face shine on you
and be gracious to you;
the LORD turn his face toward you and give you peace."

NUMBERS 6:24–26 NIV

Lord, you are the best gift-giver in the entire universe.
It makes sense when I consider that all of creation is
your design. When you dreamed up this world, I wonder
what you saw in the clarity of your creativity. There is no
question of your investment; you gave everything so we
could rightly know you in all your lovingkindness.

Today, bring revelation that comes from seeing you in a
new and fresh way. Lord, shine on me with the light of your
grace; look toward me with your kindness and grant me
peace. Bless me with your support and keep me safe in
the space you inhabit. You are everything I long for. There
is nothing of more worth than you. There is so much to be
grateful for; where do I start? In your life, I have found my
own. I had nothing lasting to live for before; thank you for a
hope and a future that is bright.

Who can you bless today?

All My Desire

Think about the things of heaven,
not the things of earth.

COLOSSIANS 3:2 NLT

Infinite One, when my eyes are focused on the pebbles in my shoe, it is easy to lose sight of the bigger picture of life. You see the challenges coming head-on; oh, how easily I get sidetracked by them. Lord, in heartbreak, confusion, and pain, I find that my thoughts hover close to the earth, close to the wounds that have not healed. I know there is grace for these seasons.

When your kingdom feels far off and it's hard to imagine what the things of heaven are, I will look to your Word. Surely, I will find all I'm looking for in your life, Jesus. I am grateful that you taught us to pray "on earth, as it is in heaven," not, "in heaven where we escape earth." Your kingdom come, Lord, to my life and my thoughts, as it already is in heaven. This is a divine mystery: your eternal presence dwelling in a temporal place. Even so, Lord, come.

What heavenly values do you think most about?

A Giving Heart

In all things I have shown you that by working hard in this way we must help the weak and remember the words of the Lord Jesus, how he himself said, "It is more blessed to give than to receive."

ACTS 20:35 ESV

Gracious God, you are so generous. May I follow the example you set in freely giving of my resources and time to serve others. You do not hold back from me, so let me serve others kindly, remembering whose lead I'm following. You know the tendency of my heart to receive freely and to store those things up, though I'm not naturally quick to give things away. As I intentionally follow your precedent, may it become more natural. I have, after all, been given a portion that comes out of the overflow of your heart. I know there is more where it came from.

May I not grow tired in serving others, building them up so they may have courage to turn around and do the same when they are able. Knowing that you are abundant in mercy and rich in compassion, I certainly won't hold back either of those. As I pour out in service, I trust that when I come to you, you will fill me up again every single time.

What can you give away more of on a regular basis?

It Is You

"The Helper, the Holy Spirit, whom the Father will send in My name, He will teach you all things, and bring to your remembrance all that I said to you."

JOHN 14:26 NASB

Holy Spirit, you are the best companion I could ever ask for. Your presence brings with it the fruit of the kingdom. Peace that passes understanding fills my heart and mind when you are near. Your love that casts out every fear is tangible with your touch. Joy springs from the depths of my soul. You hold all the wisdom I could ever look for. You're the best teacher. You don't forget a word of truth; nothing slips from your mind.

Helper, I trust you to guide me in every twist and turn in this life. Your support keeps me together when I would otherwise fall apart. You are like the wind, bringing refreshing to my sun-scorched soul. You are like water in a dry desert, reviving my body. You are like honey on my tongue, bringing sweetness to the ordinary. And you are so much more! I am so grateful for your friendship. Without you, I would not know the depth of the Father's love. Thank you for your presence in my life.

How do you see the work of the Holy Spirit in your life?

The Same Wall

I begged the Lord three times
to take this problem away from me.

2 CORINTHIANS 12:8 NCV

God of mercy, hear my cries when I call out to you. You see the struggle that I keep banging my head against the wall about; I'm so tired of it! I cannot wish it away with all my power, and I can't seem to shake it, all the same. I need you to bring breakthrough. I've tried on my own to conquer this, and I just can't. God, don't ignore me, please! I need your help to not get stuck in a cycle of shame. I need your help. Period.

Come, Lord, and meet me in the middle of this. I won't keep you on the outskirts of my problem. I invite you to come and do what only you can do. If there is something more to this that I'm not seeing, show me. I surrender to you, God. Give me the grace to do whatever it takes— whatever you ask—in order to get through this, to overcome this.

Is there a struggle that is hard for you to shake?

Surrender Again

My child, give me your heart,
and let your eyes observe my ways.

PROVERBS 23:26 NRSV

Father, I come into your grace-filled presence with an open heart today. I want to be like you, for I know that you are indescribably good. I offer you my heart and all that is in it. Have your way. As I surrender to you again today, I trust that you will give me eyes to see you as you are. If I surrender to you but I don't obey you, what's the point?

Lord, you are worthy of my every hope. As I look at your life, Jesus, I see love laid down and poured out at every juncture. How could I keep this love to myself, when you so freely put it on display for all that would open their eyes to see? You can have it all. Every single part of my life. I won't hold back from you because you never hold back from me.

What can you lay on the altar of surrender?

Compassionately

Jesus, when He came out, saw a great multitude and was moved with compassion for them, because they were like sheep not having a shepherd. So He began to teach them many things.

MARK 6:34 NKJV

Lord, your heart of kindness toward me is incomprehensible. You deal with me so gently; you see my great need and rush to meet it. You do not use intimidation or scare-tactics. Fear is not a force you use to keep me in line. You are so much better than the rulers of this world. Even the best ones fall short in wisdom and loving-kindness. You teach me out of the overflow of a heart of compassion, wanting me to really know you.

Thank you, Lord, for modeling sympathetic responsiveness; you don't hold signs that condemn me; you love me to life with your welcoming, warm embrace and a voice that kindly reminds me who I am. May I be rooted and grounded in this kind of mercy, operating in the same way that you do. When I am tempted to respond to others with quick judgment or dismissal, remind me of how you never do that with me, and fill my heart with compassion.

When was the last time compassion moved you to do something?

Resource of Hope

Encourage the hearts of your fellow believers
and support one another, just as you have already
been doing.

1 THESSALONIANS 5:11 TPT

Great God, you have every resource at your disposal. When
I am running close to empty, I know that you have what
I need to be filled up. What a wonderful open invitation!
Even so, you have set us in families and communities; I
am so incredibly grateful for the support of my brothers
and sisters in the kingdom. When I am discouraged, I
find solace in their company; when I feel alone and I
reach out, I realize that my situation is not isolated. I find
encouragement that my heart needs in sharing life: the
struggles, victories, and everything in between.

Thank you for flesh and blood spiritual family that can
support me in my weaknesses; as I learn to love like you,
Father, the road is bumpy but worth it. I am grateful for
the hope that grows in me as I watch others' prayers being
answered. As we call on your name together, you reach out
and encourage us with each other. What a wonder. When
the going gets tough, as it does sometimes with family,
keep us bound together in your love that perseveres.

*How does being with other believers strengthen
your hope in the Lord?*

Gratuitous Love

By grace you have been saved through faith; and that
not of yourselves, it is the gift of God; not as a result of
works, so that no one may boast.

EPHESIANS 2:8–9 NASB

Good Father, thank you for your love that you give without
reservation. You don't hold back, in fear that we won't
respond in the same way. You're not insecure in how you
reveal your affection. Thank you that the same can be said
of your great grace. You have not given a limited amount of
love to the first few responders; no, you have a plethora to
give—more than enough for every person who has ever lived.

Thank you, Jesus, for the gift of your life, death, and
resurrection. You did all the hard work of reconciliation so
we could know you without anything keeping us separated,
even death. Your gift that gives life to every seeking soul
will not change based on our behavior or choices. Your
love does not change its mind. Lord, thank you that I can
be sure that I'm securely found in you. Your grace bridges
the gap of my own lack every single time.

*Are you confident that God's love covers
every one of your weaknesses?*

Exercise in Hope

Be joyful because you have hope.
Be patient when trouble comes,
and pray at all times.

ROMANS 12:12 NCV

Lord of my heart, you are dearer to me than anything else on this earth. When storms and trials wreak havoc on my comfort, pull me back into shore with the lighthouse beacon of your love. I don't want to be tossed around, wondering where you went as the waves crash over me. Flood my mind and heart with your peace that passes all understanding today. Hope is not lost.

Lord, let the light of your face shine on me and bring me the serenity of your presence. There is no one like you, who calms the tumultuous waves and brings healing to incurable diseases. You stand alone in strength, and I am connected to the same power that raised the dead. I know that when I pray to you, you will answer. I am not a victim to the troubles that inevitably meet me at my door. You are greater, and I cling to you. You are the hope and joy of my life in every situation.

Where does your hope come from?

Compared to Glory

I consider that our present sufferings are not worth comparing with the glory that will be revealed in us.

ROMANS 8:18 NIV

Faithful One, I cannot forget that as I walk in the way of Jesus—the path of love—suffering will be a part of it. I remember that Jesus did not say "if trials come" but "when trials come." Lord, I hold onto you in every season of my soul, knowing that you are the same yesterday, today, and forever. Keep me close to your heart in the trials, that I wouldn't lose hope. Whatever troubles I face are known to you, and you are bigger than them all. Let your glory be revealed in the way I continually choose to submit my life to you, no matter what popular opinion is.

I know that when you return, the glory of your kingdom and your people will outshine the sun, but while I await that day, give me grace to run this race with the perseverance of one whose eyes are fixed on the finish line. There is no greater glory than your life in mine.

What happens to your heart and hopes in suffering?

Turn Away

No temptation has overtaken you except such as is common to man; but God is faithful, who will not allow you to be tempted beyond what you are able, but with the temptation will also make the way of escape, that you may be able to bear it.

1 CORINTHIANS 10:13 NKJV

Abba, your great grace fills my life with the goodness of who you are. Spirit, you keep me in check, even as you pour out the fruit of the kingdom of heaven. You have been faithfully present with me in every season, and I will keep remembering your loyal love that never lets go. Faithful One, when I am tempted, show me the way out of it, so I can stand up under it, that the weight of it wouldn't overtake me.

Thank you that I don't need to be ashamed of temptation, being enticed is not a sin. You know the pull of it, Jesus. You were tempted in every way and yet did not give in. Give me the strength to turn to you instead of yielding to the compulsion that would lead me into a cycle of sin and shame. I can rely on you to strengthen me to turn away. Let self-control be a product of the Spirit's work in my life.

When you are tempted, what tools keep you from giving in?

Constant

This change of plans greatly upset Jonah,
and he became very angry.

JONAH 4:1 NLT

Constant One, your character never changes. You are
consistent in the way you lavishly love; of that, there is no
doubt. Lord, keep me solid on the firm foundation of your
compassionate kindness that overlooks offenses and longs
for others to be reconciled to you, that they may live in the
freedom of your joy over their lives. When you interrupt my
plans and schedule with impressions of compassion, I pray
for the grace to go with it. People are always more important
to you than making sure to-do lists are checked off.

Lord, may I always leave room and make space for your
Spirit to change my agenda. You always know better
anyway. I don't want to miss a moment of what you're
doing; keep my heart soft and flexible to move with you
and to not stay tied down to my own will and way. Your
intentions always supersede my own. I yield to your
leadership in my life.

How do you react when your plans are changed?

My Endurance

Since we are surrounded by so great a cloud of witnesses, let us also lay aside every weight, and sin which clings so closely, and let us run with endurance the race that is set before us.

HEBREWS 12:1 ESV

Mighty God, you possess all the strength I need to keep going when all I want to do is give up. I am so grateful that you haven't given up on me, but oh, how I am tempted to throw in the towel sometimes. Today, I offer my weak heart to you. Fill it with your love that gives power. You are the source of energy that turns the lights on and keeps everything running. Without you, my heart would be completely dark.

I know that I walk the same path that others have treaded; I am surrounded by many who have gone before. With that in mind, I throw off everything that opposes your kingdom's values and the selfish sins that keep dragging me down, and I pick up speed, running this race of life. Thank you, Lord, that the obstacles will not take me out. With you as my coach, I will keep on going.

What is weighing you down and holding you back as you journey through this life?

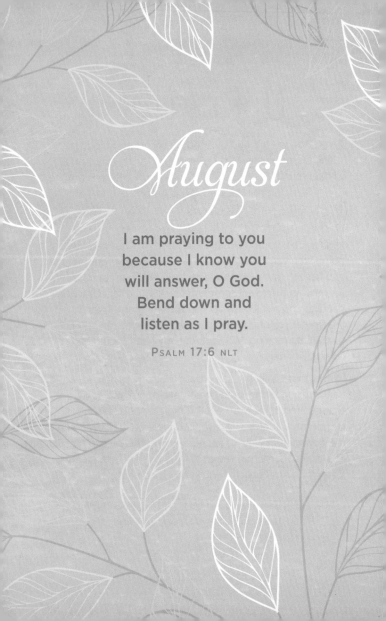

August

I am praying to you
because I know you
will answer, O God.
Bend down and
listen as I pray.

PSALM 17:6 NLT

Lead Me

> "Father, if you are willing, take away this cup of suffering. But do what you want, not what I want."
>
> LUKE 22:42 NCV

Great God, you are the leader of my life and I submit my will to yours. I don't want to walk through hardship; I wish my choices were easier, that there wasn't pain involved. But I see that I cannot avoid discomfort in this life. When choosing to walk the path of love in your footsteps looks like dying, fill my heart with courage. I would rather not suffer; I don't want to endure the grief of losing that which I love. But you see the bigger picture.

When I don't understand, I will trust in you. When I can't see the benefit of obedience, still I will choose you. I cannot outrun the inevitable. As I walk through anguish and heartache, I trust that you will be near. I need you to be. Lead me, and I will follow. When my heart starts to build up walls of protection, take them down, brick-by-brick, with your loving-kindness. Let me not forget that you share in my suffering even as I share in yours.

*Are you resisting the Lord's leadership
in any area of your life?*

Suffering

Heal me, O Lord, and I will be healed;
Save me and I will be saved,
For You are my praise.

JEREMIAH 17:14 NASB

God of comfort, you are the presence that sustains my life.
You are my healer; I need your healing touch. You have
been faithfully present with me all the days of my life.
There was not a moment that you did not see me right
where I was. When I look at my life, I see your fingerprints
of grace all over it. Still, I can't pretend to not see the
suffering—the painful moments when I endured what no
one should. Give me eyes to see you in these parts too.

Lord, let my heart receive the healing and restoration it
so desperately needs. I trust that you will answer even if
the thought of these answers now seems impossible or
insufficient. I don't hide the questions from you, knowing
that you see them anyhow. I have experienced the power
of your love in so many areas. I now want to experience it
in these hidden places. I give you my heart; do your holy
healing work in me.

Will you let God into your hidden suffering?

With Patience

If we hope for what we do not see,
we wait for it with patience.

ROMANS 8:25 NRSV

Faithful One, the mark of your loyal love is all over my life. I could not deny that your power has moved in and through me in many ways. You speak and the lights come on. You move and my heart feels as if it could fly. In the mundane, I see you. I see you in the way the flowers bloom in the spring, growing swiftly after the rains. I see you in the way children readily forgive, just wanting peace and the joy of restored relationship.

As I count the ways I have seen your faithful character at work in my life, the answered prayers and desires, I can't help but be filled with courage as I look toward the future. My hope is in what I cannot see, yet my faith is in the one whose mark is all over my life. Lord, may I be patient in hope, knowing that your timing is perfect. Thank you that I don't need to make this happen. I rest in your unfailing love that carries me through.

What do you do when your patience is running thin?

Wise Enough

Blessed is the one who perseveres under trial because,
having stood the test, that person will receive
the crown of life that the Lord has promised
to those who love him.

JAMES 1:12 NIV

Helper, you are the strength I need to face the most
difficult situations in my life. I am tired of trying to get
through with my own limited resources. I can't do this on
my own. When the pressure of life's demands threatens to
crush me under their weight, be the lifter of my burdens.
It doesn't matter what the weather of life looks like, you're
always prepared. My life is linked to yours; I pull from your
power and use it.

I know that with you I can face any trial that comes. I
need your presence to fill me with everything I lack in the
moment. I know that I can persevere with you feeding me
the strength I need. Without you, I have no hope to get
through; I'd already have given up. You make me resilient.
Thank you for your help at every juncture. You fill me with
courage to keep on.

*What do you need today to keep persevering
in areas that you've been losing strength?*

These Dreams

Take delight in the Lord,
and he will give you the desires of your heart.

PSALM 37:4 NRSV

God of all my hope, I can't hold back from you. Today, I readily share with you the dreams that have been simmering in my heart. Those that have been on the backburner are ready for your attention. Whatever desires are filled, and those left to simmer a bit longer, know that I delight in you, my King. Your ways are beautiful, and your attention to detail is unmatched. I trust you with every longing and dream, knowing you are not dismissive of your children. I have known your faithful love in my life, and I will continue to see your goodness show up in immeasurable ways. I am sure of it.

Lord, you do not teach me to ignore my own heart. You welcome me to your table, that I would bring all of me to it. Today, as I pour out my dreams like I would to a trusted friend, I know that you hear me. Not only that, but you dream with me. You are so good.

What desires can you bring before God today, letting him share in both the longing and the dreaming?

As I Love

"To you who are willing to listen, I say, love your enemies! Do good to those who hate you. Bless those who curse you. Pray for those who hurt you."

LUKE 6:27-28 NLT

Kind Father, you are overflowing in love to all. You do not show favoritism in the measure you dole out to each. Jesus, when I am being flattened by the weight of unmet expectations in relationships, let me remember your life! Some of your closest friends denied and deserted you, and your enemies put you to death. Even so, you lovingly offered forgiveness for each—even those who hated your guts.

Lord, I will follow your humble example. Keep my heart right when offense rears up and I want to get even instead of laying down my rights to retaliation. I am willing to be changed by you, God. You always know the best route for love. Let me not forget that it mostly looks like self-sacrifice. May my heart remain willing to be led by you through thick and thin, mercifully offering what may never be reciprocated. You are worth it.

Can you choose to replace the hate in your heart with love or at least the willingness to love?

No Reason

God has not given us a spirit of fear,
but of power and of love and of a sound mind.

2 TIMOTHY 1:7 NKJV

Beautiful One, I know that in you I have access to everything I need for life. There is nothing I could have need of that you do not have within the abundance of your kind character and generous kingdom. When I feel the grip of fear squeezing my heart, threatening to buckle my knees and send me sprawling, I will declare your Word that says fear is not my inheritance. It is a liar and an intimidator; it cannot take away your power in my life, unless I allow it to lead me. But I will say it now, and whenever it needs to be repeated, fear is not my leader.

You are my good Father. You have given me a spirit of power, of love, and of a sound mind. When my mind begins to race with fearful possibilities that have no roots in reality, I will stop them in their tracks. Thank you for your Spirit that brings life and calms the chaos of dread. You are so good.

When fear intimidates you, how do you combat it?

Help Me

"The LORD will fight for you,
and you have only to be silent."

EXODUS 14:14 ESV

Defender, your power to fight on my behalf is more than sufficient. You are perfect in your ways. You don't fight dirty, but you also know how to make the enemy flee. It is so hard to not come to my own defense when I've been wrongly accused; I just want them to know how wrong they are! But what good would that do? They wouldn't listen to me, anyway. I can trust you to represent me well and rightly; you won't distort the truth and you won't try to cover the reality to protect anyone's ego. You are the most qualified defender there is, and you never fail.

Help me to rest in your ability, Lord. May I keep my mouth shut and keep living the way I have been—for you. I trust that you see the truth of the matter, and you will make all things right.

*Can you let God into the place of defending you
instead of trying to do it on your own?*

Unshakable

"The steadfast of mind You will keep in perfect peace,
Because he trusts in You."

ISAIAH 26:3 NASB

Almighty One, you are the rock that my life is built upon.
When storms come, my foundation will not be moved; it
can't be washed away. My mind is set on you, the author
and perfecter of my faith. You keep me steady through
the ups and downs of life, over the hills and through the
valleys. As long as I trust in you, your peace is my portion.
I don't have to go searching for stillness because it is
readily accessible right here and now.

Thank you, Lord, for your love that is unwavering in its
intensity. You keep me insulated in the affections of your
heart. I will keep my mind fixed on you, resolute to the very
end. Thank you for your grace that fills in every crack in my
armor. You turn my deficits into stores of your goodness.
I can't stop marveling at your wonderful ways.

Where does your trust lie?

Growing Wiser

The wisdom from above is always pure, filled with peace, considerate and teachable. It is filled with love and never displays prejudice or hypocrisy in any form.

JAMES 3:17 TPT

God of all wisdom, your understanding is unmatched. Your insights have pinpoint accuracy. Who else has that type of track record? Your wisdom is saturated with the fruit of the Spirit, giving life to all who taste its bounty. As I seek you, may I be filled with your knowledge that goes above and beyond any that I could find in even the most prestigious universities on earth. When I look for you, I find you. I don't have to pay you a fee for your time; how unlike this world's ways.

Your pure wisdom gives me life as I submit to your advice. I could not find a better counselor; you are the best there is. You are unbiased and generous. Oh, how I want to be more like you. As I know you more, it is much easier to spot those who have no idea what they're talking about. May I stay close to you, leaned into your love, submitted to your heart, and always ready to respond. I love you.

What does wisdom look like in your life?

Enough Today

In all circumstances take up the shield of faith,
with which you can extinguish all the flaming darts
of the evil one.

EPHESIANS 6:16 ESV

All-sufficient One, you provide me with everything I need in you. When I thought I had exhausted your help, you reached out and lifted me up, showing me that you never fail. I will face every challenge with the confidence of your presence in me. I won't let discouragement cloud my vision of you. Lord, as I walk this life with you by my side, I will not fear falling further than your grasp. You keep me steady; your arm supports me and gives me the strength I don't have on my own.

In every situation, I will keep the armor of faith firmly fastened to my being. May I continue to lean into you, depending on your gracious mercy to keep me safe when the arrows of the enemy are flying around me. You have faithfully come through more times than I can count, and I know you won't stop now.

What does your faith provide you with today?

Burning Joy

"Go your way, eat the fat and drink sweet wine and send portions of them to those for whom nothing is prepared, for this day is holy to our LORD; and do not be grieved, for the joy of the LORD is your strength."

NEHEMIAH 8:10 NRSV

Lord, your gracious mercy is always enough. It provides exactly what I need when I need it. In you, I find my greatest joy. I can't help but overflow with delight when I consider your faithful love in my life. When I have plenty, may I rejoice in the abundance and give away more than I keep to myself. When I have little, let me be filled with the joy that I have what I need. Look how you provide. Why would I worry about tomorrow when you so graciously give all that I need today?

Lord, may I grow in generosity as I observe your own openhandedness in my life. Instead of storing up a wealth that moths and rust could destroy, may I delight in liberally giving to those who are in need. Let my heart always be grateful for your provision, never taking it for granted. You are indescribably good to your children. I'm so thankful!

Which characteristic of God brings you joy today?

Everything

"You will seek me and find me when you seek me with all your heart."

JEREMIAH 29:13 NIV

Father, you are so incredibly accessible. Thank you for not hiding your presence from me. You say that when I seek you with all my heart, I will find you. I have sought, and I have found. I haven't lost you. You do not pull away in my questioning. You don't turn your back on me when I'm not sure what to believe. You are the source of all life and all wisdom. You don't withdraw your counsel from those who ask for it.

Lord, you know my present state, where my mind and heart are in this moment. I don't have to pretend to be in a different state of mind. I come to you honestly, just as I am. I ask that you meet me here with all that you are. I don't want to hold back from you. You want a true and honest heart, and that is what I offer you today. Breathe your breath of life over me, removing the dust of the world's wishes and ways. You are always better than I expect you to be. Come and blow my expectations out of the water again.

Will you be honest with where your heart is today?

Humble Servant

"If anyone slaps you on one cheek, offer him the other cheek, too. If someone takes your coat, do not stop him from taking your shirt."

LUKE 6:29 NCV

Almighty God, you are the epitome of greatness. All-powerful, all-knowing, you are the alpha and omega. In you all things were created, and in you all things will find their completion. There is nothing in this world—physical or spiritual—that is too difficult for you to overcome. You are the king of all. And yet, you became the example of what it means to be a humble servant. When you were accused, slandered, and beaten, you did not fight back. Surely, if you did, no one could take you.

Your great love caused you to lead us into a revolution of compassion. Our strength is not found in what we gain in fighting but what we gain in laying down our lives for others. How opposite this is to the world's ways! When I am tempted to assert power over others in your name, may I be convicted to my very core. In your name, I will lay down my rights and offenses so I can love no matter the cost. Give me grace to live like you, Jesus.

Do you assert your rights over others, or do you follow Jesus' humble example?

Distant Meaning

You are a chosen generation, a royal priesthood, a holy
nation, His own special people, that you may proclaim
the praises of Him who called you out of darkness into
His marvelous light.

1 PETER 2:9 NKJV

God of all, you put everything you have into the
redemption of your people. Your love knows no bounds;
there are no limits to the compassion you pour out on your
people. You called me out of darkness into your glorious
light—the light of your face where there are no shadows.
The mystery of your great love tore down the fences of
national, ethnic, and economic boundaries, opening the
gates of your kingdom so all may enter.

Lord, you are faithful in your leadership. There are so
many areas that I don't understand, so many things that
are too complex for me to figure out alone. However, your
character remains consistent; your goodness cannot be
hidden by technicalities. I submit myself to your leadership,
knowing that you are the only one who sees the whole
picture. Thank you for your marvelous mercy that ushers
me into your kingdom as your child.

What is the driving force of your life?

Equal Trust

Be strong and courageous,
all you who put your hope in the LORD!

PSALM 31:24 NLT

Yahweh, you are the ruler of all the earth. There is nothing that escapes your notice. No one can stay away from your watchful eye. I take hope in your unfailing love that is the guiding force of my life. Why would I fear tomorrow when I know that you are with me? I will take challenges head-on, knowing that you are right by my side, offering everything I need not just to get through but to overcome!

I have placed my life in the capable hands of my good Father. Why would I tremble at the thought of the unknown? I will be strong in you, filled with courage in my heart of hearts. You're never going to lead me astray or leave me alone. My hope will grow in the soil of your faithfulness. The light of your love builds my strength to stand when the winds of change come. In you, I will not be shaken.

Do you trust God to take care of you?

With Help

I will instruct you and teach you the way you should go;
I will counsel you with my eye upon you.

PSALM 32:8 NRSV

Counselor, you are the one I turn to when I am not sure which path to take. You are faithful in instruction, always offering your wisdom when I ask. Your Word is full of your simple approach to life. Though not easy, your plan always yields the fruit of your kingdom. Above all else, I want to be found in you. You are indescribably good. You see the choices before me, and give me the wisdom I need to choose the way that aligns most with who you are and who you've called me to be.

I don't have to fear that you will misdirect me. You don't withhold advice when I ask for it, so with faith I believe I will have the assurance I need to move forward in wisdom and peace. I'm so grateful that my path is not set in concrete. There is so much more grace available than I anticipate. I take hope in knowing every success and every failure is an opportunity to find you in the middle of it. You never give up, so neither will I.

What do you need direction for right now?

Hope Wins

We also have joy with our troubles, because we know
that these troubles produce patience. And patience
produces character, and character produces hope.

ROMANS 5:3–4 NCV

Lord, when I am facing troubles of many kinds, fill me
with your presence that brings me peace. I don't want to
despise the challenges, as I'm prone to do. Instead, as I
bear the burdens of trials along with you, I find that my
soul is learning endurance. As my tolerance grows so does
my honor. I cling to you through storms and sunny days.

In the growth of my character, I find that new hope has
sprung to life. Where did that come from? What joy I
find as I look back on the trial that I thought could do
nothing but bring me pain and tear me down and see it
has brought new confidence in your faithfulness. You are
so good to me. With anticipation, I look forward to the
fruit that will grow because you have sowed your seeds of
goodness in every season.

Where do you see the fruit of hope in your life?

Rest Awhile

All who have entered into God's rest have rested from their labors, just as God did after creating the world.

HEBREWS 4:10 NLT

Abba, you are the love that brings my soul rest. I take my cue from you, Creator God, who took time to rest and enjoy the work of your hands after you created the world and everything in it. You have all the balance I'm looking for in my life. You are not a workaholic, and you are not lazy. You, who created me, know exactly what I need for every season of life. I will not work myself into burnout, keeping the endless checklist of what needs to be done as a guilt-motivator in the back of my mind.

Lord, you are so much better than that. Teach me to make margin in my life, instilling rest as a value. I know that as I take respite in you, enjoying life without the constraints of work for one day a week, I will find the refreshment I need to keep going with a full tank. May I develop the habit of rest, becoming counter-cultural in how I set aside the hustle and find my repose in you.

When was the last time you spent a whole day doing what was restful?

If I Quit

If we are joined with him in his sufferings, then we will reign together with him in his triumph. But if we disregard him, then he will also disregard us.

2 TIMOTHY 2:12 TPT

Everlasting Father, you are my sustainer in every season. Let me be found in you both now and at the end of my life. I don't want to stray from you, God. In the trials of life, may I be found secure in the loyalty of your love. You don't ever let go of me. May I not pull myself from your grip by refusing to stick with you in the suffering of life. You do not promise an easy life. I know this. I don't want easy, I want connection with you; you are my lifeline.

Lord, I won't pretend that I haven't wondered if a different life would be better, but I keep coming back to you. I couldn't imagine life without you, and I don't honestly want to. Upholder of my faith, you are too good for me to leave behind for temporal relief or pleasure. Lord, give me vision to see the beauty of the end goal so that even in the hard times, I will not lose all hope.

What would it cost you to give up your faith?

Let go

A time to seek, and a time to lose;
a time to keep, and a time to cast away.

ECCLESIASTES 3:6 NRSV

Son of Man, you are the example I look to for life. Your own life was lived with so much connection to the Father, so much intentionality in relationship. I want to be just like you. You are a master of knowing the seasons. Help me to follow you in every type of spiritual, emotional, and physical climate. Your character does not change based on the weather even if mine does. Let me be sensitive to the timing of the moment. I know that leaned into you, I won't miss it.

Lord, I know that there is a time to hold onto something and a time to let it go. Give me grace to know which is which. I feel your grace extending an invitation that even in letting go, it is making room to receive more of who you are. I will not be an obstinate child, holding onto something that I have outgrown simply because it is familiar and comfortable. I let go, and in doing so, make space to receive what you have to give now. Thank you for your grace that helps me to do this.

What do you need to let go of?

My Comforter

> "Take my yoke upon you. Let me teach you,
> because I am humble and gentle at heart,
> and you will find rest for your souls."
>
> MATTHEW 11:29 NLT

Comforter, I am joined to you. Your gentle and humble heart draws me in every single time. Why would I resist your presence when it brings me the life I so desperately long for? There isn't anything that you lack. Oh God, you know when my heart is heavy with sadness. In these times, fill my heart with your love that brings relief. In your eyes, I see the reflection of my sorrow.

What a beautiful mystery, that you share in my grief not just in a "yeah, I know how you feel" kind of way; you weep with those who weep and mourn with those who mourn. My heart is overwhelmed with this solidarity. Thank you for not demeaning my grief by explaining it away. I know that I will see the rainbows of your promises, but in the middle of my heartbreak, you do not rub my face in the happiness of others. Thank you that you are present in my process. I am undone by your steadfast companionship.

Can you invite God into your pain,
daring to see where he is in it?

your Faithfulness

My covenant I will not break,
Nor alter the word that has gone out of My lips.

PSALM 89:34 NKJV

Faithful One, you are more consistent than the sunrise. Your promises do not turn up empty; you fulfill every one, even if it takes a lifetime. You don't forget what you have spoken. Even the best-intentioned parent or partner will drop the ball, but not you. Thank you for your goodness that is always accessible in your love. Your Word is like law. Once spoken, it will be. When I look at how many times in your Word you repeatedly say, "Don't be afraid" and "take courage" because you will never leave us on our own, I can't help but be encouraged in faith. You are with me. What a glorious reality!

Lord, increase my faith even more, that I would stand strong on the foundation of your strong love. You are everything I could ever need, and you are taking care of every detail of my life. I don't need to be afraid of what will come as I lean on you.

What promises of God are you standing on?

Some of Heaven

How abundant are the good things
that you have stored up for those who fear you,
that you bestow in the sight of all,
on those who take refuge in you.

PSALM 31:19 NIV

God my refuge, you are the shelter I run to in the storms of life. You are never far away. I am so grateful for the safety I find in you. You can't be moved or shaken. You are the rock of my salvation—my firm foundation. You generously give out of the abundance of your goodness to all those who come to you for refuge. You don't secretly build us up, you do it plainly for everyone to see.

In your wisdom, you give everyone their portion. How great is the love you freely pour out. I am overcome by emotion when I think about your great faithfulness. I see you at work in the lives of my friends and family, and I see you so clearly in my own. In your abundant gifts, I am more than satisfied. I will not be stingy in doling out my own. Thank you for the consistent glimpses of heaven in the gifts you place in my life.

*What gifts has God deposited in your life
that are pure goodness?*

Protect My Heart

Do not be fooled: "Bad friends will ruin good habits."

1 CORINTHIANS 15:33 NCV

Lord, I submit my life to your leadership. I don't want to be influenced by the ways of this world, lowering the standard of the quality of my life. I know that your ways, though not easy, are better than my own. Let me be purposeful in who I spend my time with, surrounding myself with those who love you. I see the value in considering who gets to influence me.

Let me take into account the fruit of my relationships, letting those who are builders and refiners have ready access. Your wisdom speaks to every area of my life. I won't keep my friendships outside of the realm of your input. May I value the integrity of my heart and life enough to be picky about those who get most of my time. Thank you for the freedom to choose this. I don't have to live arm-in-arm with those who don't treat others with kindness and respect. I will not feel guilty for putting up necessary boundaries in relationships. Protect my heart as I make these choices.

Who do you need to allow less access to your life?

Paved Road

Without consultation, plans are frustrated,
But with many counselors they succeed.

PROVERBS 15:22 NASB

Holy One, in you is an abundance of wisdom. I will not be fooled into thinking that I can or should figure everything out on my own. Why put that kind of pressure on myself? Lord, as I look for wise input in my decisions, I ask that there would be a thread of commonality that speaks truth to my situation. I'm not looking for easy answers or paths; I'm looking for the best options. I know that as I go to trusted counselors, friends, and mentors I will find the refinement that my plans need.

Thank you for your consistent grace; when I am not sure who to turn to for help, would you place wise people in my path? I know that valuable advice comes from all kinds of sources. I will keep an open mind as I consult with others, trusting that you will not let me be led astray.

*What plans have you been devising on your own
that could benefit from outside perspective?*

Words of Life

"I tell you, on the day of judgment you will have to give an account for every careless word you utter; for by your words you will be justified, and by your words you will be condemned."

MATTHEW 12:36–37 NRSV

King of Kings, your judgments are wise and your perspective perfect. I align myself with you and your kingdom again today. I invite you to remove everything that stands against your character: your holy love that is full of grace, truth, peace, and mercy. Where I have become complacent in the words that leave my mouth like a torrent, I ask for a check-in with holy fear to consider the possible impact of my carelessness. I repent for the ways my words misrepresent you to those around me.

God, I struggle with the line of wanting to be real and seeking to honor you. Help me to have a guard over my mouth so I think about what I say before it leaves my tongue. I don't want to wound people with thoughtless words that do nothing for your kingdom. I know you readily give to all who ask, and I am asking for your help.

Do you consider the impact of your words before you speak them?

It Makes Sense

He heals the brokenhearted
and bandages their wounds.

PSALM 147:3 NLT

Healer, you bind up the brokenhearted and heal our bleeding wounds. You don't turn away, queasy at the sight of the bleeding and broken. You are quick to help. Lord of my affections, would you touch my heart with the healing power of your love? I cannot heal myself; you know how I've tried. There is no one like you. Even the most skilled doctors don't have the answers to every ailment. But you have the solution for every sickness.

Heal my body, God! I trust in your unfailing love to meet me in my weakness. You do what others can't; who else can heal a broken heart? I've never known another to do it. I offer you every broken part of me—every physical, emotional, and spiritual piece of me that is not whole, and I invite you to do your healing work. I need you. I know I will rejoice in you in the end.

Is there a heartbreak that you can invite the Lord into?

Wise Words

Do not believe every spirit, but test the spirits, whether they are of God; because many false prophets have gone out into the world.

1 JOHN 4:1 NKJV

Infinite One, your power knows no limits or boundaries. Your wisdom constantly counsels me, leading me into truth. Your love follows me all the days of my life. I could go on about how you lead, love, and strengthen me in every area of life. Lord, I am thankful that you give us the ability to distinguish the spirits behind every movement. I won't fool myself into thinking that a feeling is enough; the fruit of a life or ministry is the clue to know whether it's aligned with you or not.

God, as I seek you, I will not be afraid of falling prey to false doctrine or prophets, knowing that you are the ultimate leader. Help me to keep your law of love in mind when I test the fruit of different ministries. Thank you that in you I know the truth, and the truth sets me free.

Do you trust that you are able to test whether a teaching is from God or not?

For Good

We are convinced that every detail of our lives is continually woven together to fit into God's perfect plan of bringing good into our lives, for we are his lovers who have been called to fulfill his designed purpose.

ROMANS 8:28 TPT

Holy God, you are so intentional in your leadership. You expertly weave the tapestry of my life into a beautiful, gallery-worthy piece of art. I know I can trust that you are working every detail of my life for my benefit and for your glory. I won't worry about anything being wasted because you use it all. I love you for all the care and attention to detail you have. You use every scrap of my life and weave it in, not throwing any part out.

Master Designer, your eye for how individual parts add to the bigger picture is without rival. I am so privileged to be your workmanship. Thank you for using my life for a greater purpose; I cannot rightly express the depths of gratitude I feel. As the work of your hand, your signature is all over my life. No one can deny it! What a beautiful point of view.

Looking at the bigger picture of your life,
do you see the thread of God's goodness?

My Intercessor

In the same way the Spirit also helps our weakness;
for we do not know how to pray as we should, but the
Spirit Himself intercedes for us with groanings
too deep for words.

ROMANS 8:26 NASB

Spirit of God, when I don't know the words to pray, fill in with your own expression of what is in my heart. I am so grateful that I can rely on you in every moment; you take my weakness and breathe your life that brings strength. You bring light to every dark situation. There is no problem too tough or trial too rough for you to turn it on its head. I love that about you! When I am at a loss for words, it's all the same to you, because you see straight to the heart of me.

Spirit, intercede on my behalf. Pray what I don't even know how to. You are my ever-present help in time of need, expressing the needs that seem too great to meet. Nothing is too difficult for you. Thank you for your endless willingness and strength to pick up where I leave off. Right now, I quiet myself before you and ask for your language to take over my own.

*Do you trust that the Holy Spirit makes up
the difference when you don't know what to say?*

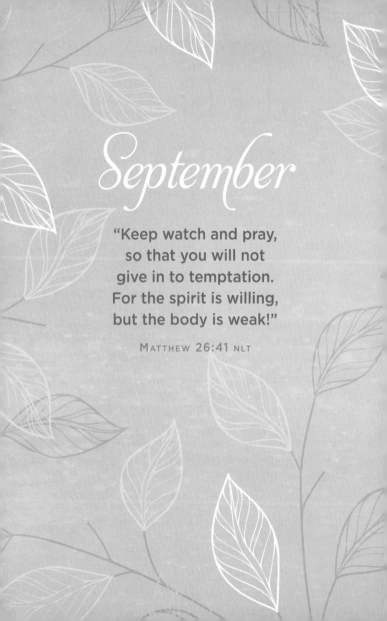

September

"Keep watch and pray,
so that you will not
give in to temptation.
For the spirit is willing,
but the body is weak!"

MATTHEW 26:41 NLT

Hope in the Light

"Behold, I am doing a new thing;
now it springs forth, do you not perceive it?
I will make a way in the wilderness
and rivers in the desert."

ISAIAH 43:19 ESV

Restorer, you are an expert at taking worn-out, old things and making them new. You always make a way when there seems to be no option; you form oases in the desert. Who is there like you, who turns mountain paths into treasure troves? You are incredible! Keep my mind set on you. When I start to forget how wonderful you are in your constant creativity, reveal your goodness in my life in a new way.

God, I submit my life to you and harness myself to you. Your leadership is unlike any other I've ever known. My humble heart is joined to your reliable love. Have your way in my life and touch each part with your resurrection power. When I am stuck in a rut of negative thinking and patterns, I need the power of your renewal. I know you won't let me down; you are the fixer of my life.

What new thing is God doing in your life?

Brave Enough

Lying lips are an abomination to the LORD,
but those who act faithfully are his delight.

PROVERBS 12:22 NRSV

Faithful One, you are the strength of my heart. Everything you do is saturated in your love; your great affection covers all my imperfections and fills every lack with the abundance of your goodness. I cannot begin to adequately thank you. You are true to your Word. You are exactly who you say you are. You don't change with the wind. I won't wake up one day to find you are a completely different person than I knew fifteen years ago. Your constancy is staggering; your goodness, even more so. I want to live a life of integrity: honest with my words as well as my actions.

May I be true to who I am in you in every area of life, consistently showing up as myself in every situation no matter who I am around. May I be true to my word, just as you are to yours. May I never give the run-around with my words or intentions. As you are, so let me be.

What does it cost you to be honest in hard situations?

Great Things

Using the Scriptures, the person who serves God will be capable, having all that is needed to do every good work.

2 TIMOTHY 3:17 NCV

Holy One, you are worthy of all that I could ever offer you. In my life, Lord, I give you access to every part of me. You can have my heart; it is yours. I submit my mind to you. Let it be full of your peace and purity. I offer you my time. You are worthy of every moment. I give you my body. I want you to be glorified in my physical body as well as my spiritual one.

Thank you for your grace that offers everything I need in order to walk this road of life with you. I know I will have what I need at the right time because you are the source of all good things. I won't lack anything because you give freely from the abundance of your kingdom. When I am stumped as to what to do, I will look to the wisdom of your Word where I will find the keys I need. With you, all things are possible. Of that, I can be sure!

When you don't know what to do, where do you turn?

The Right Path

A man's heart plans his way,
But the Lord directs his steps.

PROVERBS 16:9 NKJV

God of all my days, you hold the keys to every problem that presents itself in my life. I don't have to worry when I am walking with you. Though I make plans, I know that the actual steps are directed by you. For that, I'm thankful. Without your wisdom to guide me, I would be lost in the details of my own strategies which fall short every time.

Whether my dreams come true or all my plans fall apart, you remain the same. Your delight in me has nothing to do with my success or output; it has everything to do with who you've created me to be, and I am not what I do for a living. It may be a reflection, but it certainly isn't where I find my worth; my worth is found in my relationship with you. Lead me on; I trust in your direction for my life.

*When things don't turn out the way you'd hoped,
do you trust that the Lord has a plan?*

One Thing

"God so loved the world that he gave his one and only Son, that whoever believes in him shall not perish but have eternal life."

JOHN 3:16 NIV

Good God, you are beautiful in the way you love. Thank you for the sacrifice of your Son that brings every person who believes eternal life. What a tremendous cost for you and incredible blessing for us. Your extravagant love is without rival; no one can match the character or magnitude of it. Your love broke even the grip of death; yours is the final word, and that word is life!

Your resurrection power is alive and well today, as it was when Jesus first rose from the dead. There is no power in all the earth or beyond that can stand up to yours. You are the victorious king, Jesus, and you reign in glory—soon for all to see. May I be found in the camp of my King when the day of his return comes. God, let me be your ally and friend until the end. Keep me close.

When you boil down your faith in Jesus to its simplest form, what does it look like?

Open Door Policy

Do not neglect to show hospitality to strangers,
for thereby some have entertained angels unawares.

HEBREWS 13:2 ESV

Good Father, you are the epitome of what it means to be hospitable. You welcome friend and foe alike with open arms and a table set with the finest foods. As you receive everyone with warmth and kindness, may I too. It is easy with friends and family, but to be warm and generous with strangers is not as natural. Fill me with a heart of love and compassion that goes beyond conventional kindness to reveal your benevolent heart.

You offer everyone a place at the table; there is no one who isn't welcome. Your home remains an open invitation. As I freely come and go with confidence, may I take generosity with me. Thank you for your open-door policy; there are no time restraints or off hours, where I'm not allowed to show up. As a dearly loved child, I know I am always welcome. Thank you that I am not a stranger in your house. As I have been loved, may I love others.

When was the last time you felt like a stranger?

Only Love

Love each other with genuine affection,
and take delight in honoring each other.

ROMANS 12:10 NLT

Compassionate One, you set the example of pure love for us to follow. It is your very nature to interact with us in the warmth of affection. As we love each other with this same conscious kindness, we reflect your character. Lord, I want to be like you in your lovingkindness. I struggle to love everyone in my life with true affection; I need your help.

Fill me with your grace that empowers me as I choose to honor others whether or not I feel like doing it. Your love constantly chooses honoring others over comfort. It is not my natural inclination, but I will practice choosing it until it becomes like second-nature. When I fail to choose love, grace is accessible. There is a multitude of opportunity in the failing and trying again. Help me to love like you do.

How does love honor others in your life?

More Like You

I pray with great faith for you, because I'm fully convinced that the One who began this glorious work in you will faithfully continue the process of maturing you and will put his finishing touches to it until the unveiling of our Lord Jesus Christ!

PHILIPPIANS 1:6 TPT

Beautiful One, you have not given up your work in me. Thank you for your love that gives me new life and renews my weary soul. You are the one who started this work in me, and you aren't going to quit and walk out on me now. I want to look more like you; as I mature in you, walking with your Spirit as my guide, I find that my nature is becoming like yours. I am so grateful for the way you love me to life over and over again. You don't grow tired of pouring out grace to those who need it.

Lord, read the thoughts of my heart that are set on you; I rely on you for every good thing. This life is a gift, and your presence is the force that continually shapes me into who you always dreamed I would be. May I become more like you with each passing day.

How do you see God's likeness showing up in you?

Adversity

"My grace is sufficient for you, for power is perfected in weakness." Most gladly, therefore, I will rather boast about my weaknesses, so that the power of Christ may dwell in me.

2 CORINTHIANS 12:9 NASB

Faithful One, as I face all sorts of trials and problems, I trust you to be the sure foundation I stand upon. You are the rock of salvation, and you won't be moved. I lean into your grace that is enough for every single area of need in my life. There is no gap that your love can't cover. There's no crater too wide that you won't cross. You are full of every good thing I could ever look for, and your love is the fulfillment of every longing.

God, you see the situations that I am facing: the relational struggles that I'm dealing with right now. I have run out of strength. I clearly feel my weakness. I need your grace, which is always enough, to empower me to continue to love in each of these instances, believing the best about others and not taking on a victim mentality. I know that you will help me see from your perspective. May I be found strong in you no matter how weak I get on my own.

What weaknesses are areas that God can empower with his strength?

Love Never Ends

A thousand years in your sight
are like a day that has just gone by,
or like a watch in the night.

PSALM 90:4 NIV

Almighty God, your love is never-ending. It is more faithful than the rising and setting of the sun. There is not a day that goes by where your great affection was absent. It's impossible. Your love is the driving force of the universe. In your presence, time is relative for you are outside of time. A thousand years is like a day gone by, and a day like a thousand years. Who can make that sort of distinction? You're amazing, Lord. What's even more amazing is that your faithful love has been present at every juncture and always will be.

When my hope starts to falter, would you remind me that my timing is not the same as yours? You're not in a hurry; you don't feel the urgency of time. Give me grace that I wouldn't feel urgency unless necessary. I will live a better life when I am aligned with your timing and not demanding my own. I trust you.

*Does the timing of God's promises affect
the love you feel from him?*

The Same Hands

"You have also given me the shield of Your salvation;
your gentleness has made me great."

2 SAMUEL 22:36 NKJV

God of all, the hands that offered to fight our battles are the same hands that gently hold us when we're vulnerable. You are strong and incredibly kind. These virtues seem at odds in modern society; although, surely, they go hand in hand. Who is there like you, who used his hands to carefully mold a woman out of a man's rib, and who also crushed his enemies with his strong right arm? You are not in conflict with yourself.

Where this mystery is still a bit too high for me to understand, I recognize that we were made in your image. We were created to be both strong and tender, so we all have that potential in us. Thank you for strength and kindness that literally goes hand-in-hand. You are so much better than you ever get credit for. Be glorified in my own hands. May they be strong to protect and gentle in nurturing.

*How does the use of your hands reflect
the character of Christ?*

No Words

They sat on the ground with him for seven days and seven nights. No one said a word to him, because they saw how great his suffering was.

JOB 2:13 NIV

Comforter, you always know exactly what to do with my grief. There are moments when I think if anyone says a thing, I'll scream. There are other times when I'm longing for a word of comfort—something, anything to break the tension of the heavy silence of sadness. Words take on a different weight in the presence of grief and suffering. Superficial well-wishes sound tinny and empty, floating off and completely missing any mark they were aiming for. Those who profess sincere truth in not knowing what to say offer the solidarity of pain while not trying to explain it away.

There is profound beauty in being able to sit with someone in their pain and suffering without offering words that try to fix what cannot be fixed. Jesus, you knew the anguish of grief. You know just how to handle it. Let me be slow to speak in the presence of great pain, and quick to sit with those who are suffering without trying to fix them.

What do you do when those you love are suffering?

When Glory Comes

We thank God!
He gives us the victory
through our Lord Jesus Christ.

1 CORINTHIANS 15:57 NCV

God of glory, you are the fulfillment of every longing heart. Jesus, your victory over death is still being celebrated. It will be forever. You made freedom possible. You broke every chain of sin and death that kept us bound. There is no more bondage because of you. Thank you for your freedom that allows me to choose my own way without the shadow of sin hanging over me.

Lord, I wouldn't go anywhere that would take me from you. I want to be found in you when you return. May I be found in you now. I am so grateful for victory. I am an overcomer in you because of the weight of your sacrifice. There is no one else like you in all the earth. Be glorified above all else! I fully submit to you. Have your way in me today.

What does the glory of victory in Jesus
look like in your life?

Brought Near

Bear one another's burdens,
and thereby fulfill the law of Christ.

GALATIANS 6:2 NASB

Compassionate Caretaker, you are the kindness that meets everyone right where they are. As I become more like you, I naturally share other's burdens more readily. I have known the blessing of friends helping me lift the weight of my problems; they give me courage to persevere in the trial. It's so much easier knowing I'm not alone in it. You are so wise in your intention to set us in families and communities. I don't know what I would do without the support of your people.

Thank you for your presence that is evident, no matter the time of day or the season of the year. Your presence in your people showing up in love for one another is a sacred expression; there is something so special in it. I am grateful for the opportunity to share in your lovingkindness that sticks with people through the trenches of life, offering support and true friendship.

*Who in your life helps you carry
the weight of hard situations?*

Abba

Whoever spares the rod hates his son,
but he who loves him is diligent to discipline him.

PROVERBS 13:24 ESV

Father, you are perfect in all your ways. You don't leave us to our own devices, hoping that we'll magically figure out what is right or wrong. You don't expect us to read your mind either. You are loving in all you do. Even your correction is done in kindness. Thank you for your love that keeps leading us back to the path of life. Your kingdom's ways are so much better than the world's, but who can know them if they are not taught. You instruct me in the customs of your kingdom with the patience of a compassionate father. I am learning to be more like you.

May my heart stay humble and soft toward you, my good Father, that I would not become hardened to think that I know it all or have arrived. I trust you to correct me and discipline me when needed, and I submit to you. I am not afraid of you; there is no reason to be.

Have you experienced God's discipline in your life?

Access to Wisdom

"Call to me and I will answer you, and will tell you great and hidden things that you have not known."

JEREMIAH 33:3 NRSV

Great Counselor, you have all the wisdom I am seeking. You have the answers to difficulties that seem impossible to resolve. I need your divine problem-solving in my life more than I need anything else today. I lay out every difficulty before you. I'm so grateful that you welcome me in; you are never distracted when I need you. I am confident that as I consult with you, you will give me all the peace I need even if there is no quick-fix.

May I never reject your wisdom that seems too simple; it doesn't have to be complex or difficult to be right. When I am looking for a step-by-step plan and you ask me a clarifying question, may I not scoff, but instead take the time to answer. I won't be surprised if the answer I'm looking for is in the prodding. Ever-present One, thank you for your constant help when I need it.

What do you need wisdom for today?

You Alone

No one is holy like the LORD!
There is no one besides you;
there is no Rock like our God.

1 SAMUEL 2:2 NLT

Almighty God, you stand alone in power. Who is like you? I marvel at your wonderful mercy that you extend to all. The depths of your love no one can discover. There is no end to the kindness that you show to your people. Good Father, I needed to be reminded of just how big you are. When I'm caught up in the details of my circumstances, it's so easy to feel like the little bumps are mountains. But when I look at your vast creation and your mindful care over each detail, I can breathe a sigh of relief.

No one can get in your way or keep me away from your loyal love. There's no obstacle too large that you can't simply flick away with your finger. With renewed perspective, I can go through my day knowing that you will take care of every detail that I overlook. The strength of your love is my greatest resource.

How can you practice shifting your perspective?

Every Chance

"I am the Way, I am the Truth, and I am the Life. No one comes next to the Father except through union with me. To know me is to know my Father too."

JOHN 14:6 TPT

Jesus, you said yourself that you are the way to the Father. To know you is to know him. When I look at your intentional life, poured out in love that chooses the honor of others over convenience, I can't help but be filled with awe and conviction. Thank you for the way you set aside your own rights so we could know the incredible lengths love would go to save us. In you is all truth. Every living thing finds lasting life in your hand.

I am so grateful for relationship with you, God. I don't know where I'd be without the assurance of your presence in my life. When other voices speak up for alternate ways to know you, keep me secure in the grip of your love that never fails. I won't falter when I follow your way. Keep me on your pathway of life.

How does knowing Jesus benefit your life?

Delight in Weakness

I take pleasure in my weaknesses, and in the insults, hardships, persecutions, and troubles that I suffer for Christ. For when I am weak, then I am strong.

2 CORINTHIANS 12:10 NLT

Faithful Father, I come to you with my tired and weary self. I am worn-down, but I know that you always accept me just as I am. You meet me in my weakness and give me your own strength to lean on. I need to lean extra hard today. What a privilege that I don't ever need to second-guess your willingness to help.

You are dependable, God, and I am extremely grateful. There are so many days I don't stop to think about your help; I just run to you, and there it is. When I am up against hard times, there is no question that your strength is enough to get me through. I don't have to push through in my own power. I let you take over, and I delight in not having to be my own rescuer.

Who do you turn to when you're weak?

All Honor

The answer is, if you eat or drink, or if you do anything,
do it all for the glory of God.

1 CORINTHIANS 10:31 NCV

Glorious God, I offer you access to every part of my life
today. You are my sustainer in every circumstance of
life. As I live for you this day, with open hands, I want
everything to be like an offering to you. Nothing is wasted,
when you're in it. When I go to the bank, I will do it for you
glory. When I go to the grocery store, I will give thanks for
the provision for food. When I play with children and talk
with friends, it all matters.

There are no noble tasks or menial tasks in your kingdom. I
will do everything with your presence in my mind and your
glory in the attitude of my heart. I have forgotten about
you in the day-to-day rush, caught up in the moment's
demands, but today, let me live with intention, partnering
with and for you in everything I do. You're so worthy.

*Do you think about the mundane
as opportunities to glorify God?*

Just Us

The faith which you have, have as your own conviction before God. Happy is he who does not condemn himself in what he approves.

ROMANS 14:22 NASB

Lord my God, you are the tether that keeps me grounded in the law of love. As I walk this road with you, let my heart stay rooted in the relationship with you—the way, the truth, and the life. May I live with the conviction of my faith as I keep my hands readily serving in the world. May my ears stay tuned to your voice, my eyes with the ability to see your love in the most unlikely places, and my heart to the compassion that calls out your name.

I remain rooted in you—the originator of my faith. I am like a tree planted by streams of living water. As I drink deeply of you, I grow and bear the fruit of your kingdom. I will stay steady in the confidence you give me as a child of God. I won't be swayed by the world's ways as long as I have you in my sights.

What fuels your faith?

Powerful Presence

You make known to me the path of life;
in your presence there is fullness of joy;
at your right hand are pleasures forevermore.

PSALM 16:11 ESV

Life Giver, yours is the kingdom, the power, and the glory.
There is no one like you in all of creation. Your powerful
presence gives me joy. There is so much pleasure in
knowing you. When I thought I had lost myself in my pain,
you brought me out into the light; there, I could clearly
see the treasures that had been hidden in darkness. You
never waste an opportunity to lavish your love on me. I am
undone at the faithfulness of your goodness in my life.

Lord, as you have freely poured out your affection over me,
how could I but turn around and give it right back? The
cycle of praise and affection is endless. You are genuine in
your adoration of your children; you draw out love within
me that I didn't even know was there. You're a master at
bringing life to everything you give attention to. Thank you
that I am one such subject.

When is the last time you felt pure joy?

Life of Integrity

For our sake he made him to be sin who knew no sin, so that in him we might become the righteousness of God.

2 CORINTHIANS 5:21 NRSV

Righteous One, who could measure up to your blameless standard? Your honorable and just character is without match in this world. Thank you for leveling the playing field for us all when Jesus came and abolished the law of sin and death. In his righteousness, we find ours—not by anything we could ever do on our own. Lord, as your child, I want to live as a reflection not just of your honorable character but also of your incredible kindness in providing a way to be reconciled to you.

I surrender myself to you again, Lord. May the way I live my life lead others into relationship with you: the King of Glory who loves them beyond their wildest imaginings. Thank you that I am blameless in you, and I can live with the confidence of your life changing my own. Be honored in my life today and every day.

What does living an honorable life mean to you?

What I Would Do

"If the world hates you,
remember that it hated me first."

JOHN 15:18 NLT

Faithful One, you laid down your life in love for everyone even those who reject you. It is hard to imagine, this far out, how anyone could have looked at your life and hated you. And yet, the longer I live, the more understandable it is as I look at the offenses and fear that lead people to hate. Jesus, you bucked religious systems and upended the status quo. You ate with sinners and hung out with fisherman and tax collectors. You befriended and honored women. You didn't live according to the religious elite's view of what it meant to be righteous.

You were a pure reflection of God's holy love for humanity. They totally missed it! If I am hated, let it be because I love too liberally for people's understanding. If they are offended, let it be because of the grace I extend to all people. I won't go wrong if I'm living like you, whether or not I'm accepted by others.

How do you react when people don't like you?

Greater Impact

Commit your work to the LORD,
and your plans will be established.

PROVERBS 16:3 NKJV

Great God, you see the plans I have formed in my head
and the details I'm working out. But you, oh Lord, are the
great orchestrator. I submit my plans for your approval.
Whatever you think is best is what I want. I will not push
my way through. Building plans that include a design flaw
will end up being a mess in the end. I submit my blueprints
to you to look over and wait for your feedback.

Master Architect, I know that your edits will be necessary
and will make the end product so much better. I know
that with your involvement, the fruit of my life will have
lasting impact. I have no desire to push my way to the
top of my field on my own, only to wake up one day to
dissatisfaction. I pour my life out for you. Fill me up along
the way.

What do you want the impact of your life to be?

The Source

All praise to God, the Father of our Lord Jesus Christ.
God is our merciful Father and the source of all comfort.

2 CORINTHIANS 1:3 NLT

God my Father, you are the source of everything I need for abundant life. You are the giver of every good thing. My portion for the day is found in you. Here I am with open hands to receive. I will not worry about what I don't have; I won't fret about it. I know your faithful hand of provision will deliver just what I need, right when I need it.

Merciful Father, you never give your children stones when they ask for bread. I won't have to eat rocks for breakfast. When I am grieved and I don't even know what to say, you fill me with the comfort of your presence. There is not one lack in my life that doesn't find its fill in the abundance of your affection. I admire you so deeply, faithful Father. I could never find another nearly as kind and pure in heart as you. I'm so thankful to be yours and to know you.

Do you believe that God has resources to meet every one of your needs?

Anchored

Let him ask in faith, with no doubting,
for he who doubts is like a wave of the sea
driven and tossed by the wind.

JAMES 1:6 NKJV

Steadfast One, you are my firm foundation—the anchor of my soul. Though storms come and waves of doubt try to toss me, you keep me grounded, tied to your truth that sets me free. Lord, let my heart be full of faith, approaching you without doubt. There is no one like you who is rich in mercy and patient in kindness. I could not find a more welcoming counselor.

You cause all my defenses to fall; every wall of self-protection comes tumbling down in the presence of your purely-motivated affection. I won't fear being lost at sea to a storm of confusion because the anchor of your love keeps me right where I need to be. We'll take up the route again once the storm has passed. How encouraging it is to know that you are never discouraged. I cling to your confidence when my own is severely lacking. If you have no doubts, then I don't need them either.

What is your anchor through the storms of life?

Meet Me

It is not yet time for the message to come true, but that time is coming soon; the message will come true. It may seem like a long time, but be patient and wait for it, because it will surely come; it will not be delayed.

HABAKKUK 2:3 NCV

God of Glory, the time is coming when all waiting will be over. It's almost incomprehensible. I can't quite imagine all things out in the light with no more mysteries or hidden motives. When the day has come and the delay is done, may I be found in you. All your promises will be fulfilled. Not one will turn up empty. I can trust that everything you're doing, you do exceedingly well. Your goodness will continue to follow me until the day of fulfillment and then all the more!

You never let go of me; I can trust your faithfulness to lead me into your kingdom. As a citizen of heaven, I ache for the long-awaited homecoming. What a glorious day it will be. As I continue in the waiting, strengthen me every day with courage and hope. I know it will all be worth it—every sacrifice, every trial, and every act of love.

What encourages you in extended periods of waiting?

Staying Focused

Love is patient, love is kind. It does not envy,
it does not boast, it is not proud.

1 CORINTHIANS 13:4 NIV

Compassionate One, you are full of love that keeps giving.
There are no shortages of your kindness. Though our
natural resources are limited, they will eventually run out.
Yours are infinitely abundant. It's too much to imagine
the endless lengths of your goodness. May my attention
continually be brought back to you. You are too beautiful
to overlook.

When I think about your ways and the indescribable
lovingkindness that saturates your every move, I can't
help but be overwhelmed by the glory of it. Your patience
reflects your great kindness. It is not manipulative, easily
angered, or full of itself. Your pure love draws me in time
and again. I can't help but let it. Why would I fight the
current of your affection? I let the waves crash over me;
you refresh me in every possible way. Here I am, Lord.
There is nowhere else I'd rather be.

*How does the abundance of God's love
influence your relationships?*

Reconciliation

"My people who are called by My name
humble themselves and pray
and seek My face and turn from their wicked ways,
then I will hear from heaven,
will forgive their sin and will heal their land."

2 CHRONICLES 7:14 NASB

Redeemer, you are the great reconciler. You mend the broken fences of relationships, opening gates of understanding that lead to unhindered fellowship. You heal the sicknesses of your people, renewing the hope of the disappointed. You send your compassionate love to comfort those who are brokenhearted. You breathe on the stagnant, blowing off the dust and revealing the purity underneath. Everything you do is done well. Your high standards are reflected in every situation you touch.

Lord, see the areas of my life that are desperate for your restoration. It is too much for me to fix; I couldn't even if I tried. But you are my help. You breathe life into every corner of my heart, soul, and body. My life is yours, and you can have access to every part. I will seek your face all the days of my life; there is no one like you.

What part of your life needs the power of the restorer?

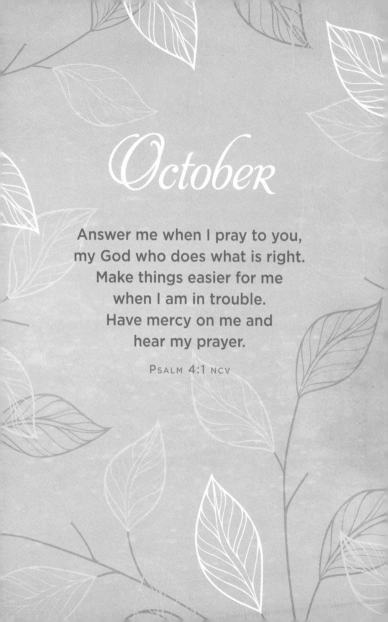

October

Answer me when I pray to you,
my God who does what is right.
Make things easier for me
when I am in trouble.
Have mercy on me and
hear my prayer.

PSALM 4:1 NCV

Guard My Heart

Set your minds on things that are above,
not on things that are on earth.

COLOSSIANS 3:2 NASB

Holy One, it's you I look to as the standard. When I look around me, all I get are mixed signals. When I consider the ways of this world, I can't help but be discouraged at the heartlessness and endless empty pursuits. Even the best things of this world come up short, when compared to your kingdom. I will set my mind on you and the values of your heart. When I do, everything becomes clearer. It's not difficult to decipher how I should live even if it doesn't answer all of the questions.

Thank you, God, for your simple but costly instructions that put lovingkindness above every other goal. It doesn't matter so much what I do if it's done with love as the driving-force and it holds to your character. I will set my heart on your kingdom as my ultimate home, so that no matter what I face, I can get through knowing that it's only temporary. Keep my mind and heart pure in motivation and intention.

*Do you ever stop to consider the source
and the fruit of your thoughts?*

Temporary

We do not look at the things which are seen,
but at the things which are not seen.
For the things which are seen are temporary,
but the things which are not seen are eternal.

2 CORINTHIANS 4:18 NKJV

Everlasting God, you are forever constant. When everything else passes away and turns to dust, you remain. Help me not to get caught up in the temporary pleasures or worries of this age that try to dictate my level of satisfaction with life. When I set my heart on the things I have or want now, when times of lack or waiting come, my heart is desperate with disappointment. But if I set my heart on who you are, and the abundance of your merciful love that is always available, my heart finds its steadiness in you.

Though disappointments come, they will not take me out. Though troubles find me, they will not dictate my peace or joy that is mine in your presence. You knew what you were doing when you gave us the Spirit who brings life to all people. What an amazing gift. I am bound to you, Lord. Fill me with the power of your constant love in a new way today.

What has been occupying your thoughts lately?

Empathy

If one part suffers, every part suffers with it;
if one part is honored, every part rejoices with it.

1 CORINTHIANS 12:26 NIV

Compassionate One, you are the light that shines on darkness. Your kindness gleams like the morning sun, waking up the world from its slumber. Lord, where I have been asleep to your concern and sympathy, shine your light of love around me, so I would see clearly. In the darkness of night, all feels heavier: the weight of sadness sinks in and the unknown feels unbearable. In the light of day, though, everything is seen clearly. Problems are usually smaller than they seemed and sunshine lifts the soul to hope.

When others are in the darkness, may I be a shining light that sticks close in love and support, not trying to fix but to share their burden. When others are celebrating the joys of dreams fulfilled, may I rejoice with them, letting go of comparison. Lord, let me reflect your constancy and community, truly sharing in the experiences of others while taking my heart before you every single day.

*What has empathy shown you
about the character of Christ?*

My Name

See, I have written your name on my hand.
Jerusalem, I always think about your walls.

ISAIAH 49:16 NCV

Good Father, I am so very grateful to be your child. You know everything about me: what gets me excited and what saddens my heart. You know my morning routine and every landmark on my route to work. You know where I go when I need a pick-me-up and what I do when I feel like I can't face the world. You are so much more than a casual observer; you know every motivation, fear, and dream. You care for every need even the ones that have completely escaped my notice. You are incredible, God.

When I spend time meditating on your inescapable goodness in my life, how could I stay away from you? Your love is amazing. My name is as familiar as Moses or David to you. That seems too wonderful to be true. But that is who you consistently prove to be—better than I expect at every turn.

How does knowing that the Father loves you
affect your thoughts about yourself?

Joy Is Medicine

A joyful, cheerful heart brings healing
to both body and soul.
But the one whose heart is crushed
struggles with sickness and depression.

PROVERBS 17:22 TPT

Great God, you are the hope of every longing heart. Just when I thought the dark night of my soul would never end, the dawn of your love broke through. I am filled with courage as you come through with your mercy again. You are the joy that springs up from deep within. When the quick feeling of relief gives way, I can feel the bubbling of delight that has had all its fears alleviated. There is pure pleasure in knowing you; you fight every battle that wages over my life. You will not let my heart be crushed completely. You are my Savior, healer, and faithful friend.

Thank you for your consistent grace that never runs out. Though I struggle to stay convinced of your support, your loyal love never wavers in the moment. I can see that now. My heart is refreshed and encouraged. Even my body feels better. You are so good, Lord. Thank you.

What brings you joy?

Get It Right

"Where your treasure is, there will your heart be also."

LUKE 12:34 ESV

Lord over all, every hope of mine is securely fastened in your perfect nature. May my confidence be based on your faithfulness and not the current state of the world. Your goodness isn't dependent on my own; what a relief. Keep my hand in yours, God, as I walk this road with you. When my eyes are fixed on you, it's easy to follow, but when my gaze drifts, I need your hand to keep me going in the right direction.

My greatest treasure is in knowing you. It is from this relationship that every good thing stems. Let me not get so caught up in achieving and receiving, or even serving, that I forget what it's all for. Fill my heart with your affection, so as I live it will flow out of everything I do. As I see your mercy at work, may it encourage my heart and keep pointing me back to your unfailing love that is always present.

What does your heart treasure?

Not Worried

Anxiety weighs down the human heart,
but a good word cheers it up.

PROVERBS 12:25 NRSV

Almighty God, the created world takes its cue from you, its maker. I look to you today as a sunflower turns its face toward the sun. I know that in you is all the strength I need. You've seen the anxieties that have been weighing me down. There are so many things outside of my control—so much that I can't fix. As I come before you, I ask that you relieve my burdens again. Be the lifter of my head. Where there has been worry, replace it with your peace that calms even the fiercest storms.

Speak your words of life over me, and I will perk up. My heart is dry and needs to drink from your refreshing waters. Come, Spirit, and fill me once again. There is no better source of encouragement or hope. You meet every need. I won't worry about today with your presence empowering me to live courageously.

*Does God's Word offer peace to your heart
and encourage you?*

Wealth of Character

Choose a good reputation over great riches;
being held in high esteem is better than silver or gold.

PROVERBS 22:1 NLT

Holy One, you are the perfect one—righteous in all your ways. As I walk in the way of love, I find opportunities to lay down my own rights and desires along the way and pick up yours. When faced with the choice of staying true to your character within me or getting everything I could ever desire, may I choose you. If I have to lie or cheat to achieve my dreams, then the price isn't worth it. May I live a life of integrity, aligning myself to your wonderful character: your mercy, kindness, justice, and peace. If I am offered a wealth of riches, but it costs me my honor, I will be the loser in the end. Keep my heart fixed on the one I am devoted to.

Jesus, I know that you faced all sorts of temptations and resisted; so can I, with your help. Thank you for always providing a way for me to stand up under the enticement of the enemy. Whether or not others speak badly about me, may their gossip have no roots in reality. I am linked to you, Lord.

What is your honor worth to you?

Call to Love

Do not rejoice when your enemy falls,
And do not let your heart be glad when he stumbles.

PROVERBS 24:17 NKJV

Merciful One, you are full of compassion that reaches out to everyone in their weakness. You do not scoff at people, not even the wicked. I think of how many times I justify the way I mock others, whether because I don't understand them or because they offend me. If I ridicule others, I am demeaning their humanity, and you never do that. Your ways are so different than those that come naturally.

Change my heart, God. I want to be more like you. You are full of kindness to all, even to those who hate you. I repent for the ways that I've demeaned others by my attitudes or actions. Give me a heart of love that offers grace to those I would naturally keep my distance from. When those who have hurt me experience the pain of rejection, humiliation, or tragedy, may my heart not react in joy at the news. Keep me humble, knowing that love is what covers my life and it is not exclusive.

*How do you react when those you find difficult
seem to get what's due?*

Strength Revealed

"Yours, LORD, is the greatness and the power
and the glory and the majesty and the splendor,
for everything in heaven and earth is yours."

1 CHRONICLES 29:11 NIV

King of Kings, the earth is longing and waiting for the
day when you will return to reign forever. Let this feel like
reality to me rather than the wishful thinking of a fairy tale
or random luck. Your presence has changed me. I've tasted
and seen the fruits of your kingdom, and I'm always left
wanting more! God, everything in this world and beyond
belongs to you. Nothing is outside of your grasp. I join with
creation in its longing. Even in the waiting, I will find that
your leadership is relevant to every decision I make.

I align myself to you and your ways. Let your greatness,
power, and glory be over and in my life, pointing directly
to the Maker as my constant help and faithful friend. Lord,
may others know who you are because of the way I choose
to live. You are the joy of my life. I am yours.

Where can you see God's power at work in your life?

The Only Judge

God is the only Lawmaker and Judge.
He is the only One who can save and destroy.
So it is not right for you to judge your neighbor.

JAMES 4:12 NCV

Mighty God, you are the only one who sees the intention of every heart. You see what is behind movements, nations, and peoples; even more acutely, you see the motivation of each person. Who can escape your watchful eye? Who can slip under the radar of your wisdom? There is no one who has ever lived that will be exempt from your thorough examination of their lives. You see it all, and you are the only one who truly understands every person and every situation.

You are the only judge. When I am tempted to pass judgment on others, remind me that I am not qualified for the job. It is your place and yours alone to judge. You are full of all wisdom and mercy, and you will do it exactly how it should be done. I will do what you have called me to: to love my neighbor and dole out mercy instead of condemnation. Let me live as one who humbly holds the power of the forgiveness I've received from you, and freely give it to others.

Do you trust that God can judge more rightly than you can?

Faithful in Little

"He who is faithful in a very little thing is faithful also in
much; and he who is unrighteous in a very little thing
is unrighteous also in much."

LUKE 16:10 NASB

Faithful One, you follow through with every promise you've
ever made. Your constancy is beyond belief; no one can
match your ability. Lord, let your character rub off on me as
I walk intentionally with you. You see the big dreams I hold
in my heart. Give me perspective to give myself to what
you've put in front of me in the same way I think I would
in my dream life. Lord, I see what I have here and now as a
gift. It's not just a training ground, though it will serve that
way, I'm sure. As you grow and test my character, may I be
found faithful to your heart.

Whether I am mowing lawns, changing diapers, or running
a company, may I faithfully follow through with my part.
May all I do be laced with the love that you have woven
through everything you touch. May my faithfulness
reflect yours, and when it falls short, may the humility of
my repentance reflect you, as well. Thank you, Lord, for
everything I have today. I will not take it for granted.

*What areas of your life have you been
writing off as unimportant?*

Honest Worship

Oh come, let us worship and bow down;
let us kneel before the LORD, our Maker!

PSALM 95:6 ESV

Lord, you are worthy of all the praise I could ever offer you. Today I bow down before you with my heart and life laid out as offerings. Come take your place in my life: the central focal point from which everything flows and takes its cues. You are Lord of my life; I will not continue my day without offering you the worship you deserve. You have been abundantly merciful and kind to me. I can't help but weep with deep gratitude for the realization of your incredible faithfulness to me.

Spirit, your revelation fills me again and again with the knowledge of the incredible greatness of the character of my God: the king of all the earth. Your mercy flows freely from your throne of grace, and I will sing of your goodness. I will shout for joy. You are indescribably good, and I won't stop bragging on your presence, available to all, for the rest of my days. I adore you.

What can you praise God for right now?

Show Me Beauty

I praise you, for I am fearfully and wonderfully made.
Wonderful are your works; that I know very well.

PSALM 139:14 NRSV

Beautiful One, the splendor of your being is reflected in your people. I see you everywhere; when I'm looking for you, I see your fingerprints on all of creation. I long to see the fullness of your glory. Oh, for that day when all things are finally made right and there are no more mysteries: no more veils or shadows. I long for wholeness that lasts not just in me but all of creation. How wonderful it will be. In the waiting, God, I will not stop searching for your beauty. I know that it is present everywhere, even the darkest caverns.

If you dig deep enough in the caves of darkness, there are jewels formed under pressure and friction. I can't go anywhere where you have not been. It is almost too much for me to know how present you are. I am so grateful. Lord, let me have eyes to see you in unexpected places today. I'm desperate for a glimpse of you.

Where do you see the reflection of God's beauty today?

Bold Confidence

It is not that we think we are qualified to do anything
on our own. Our qualification comes from God.

2 CORINTHIANS 3:5 NLT

God my strength, there is nothing I face without your love
covering me. Let me not forget that fact! I don't ever need
to rely on my own strength when your grace is always
available as a resource. I don't know why I try to do so
much on my own; I have nothing to prove.

You set the tone in this. Jesus, your radical call to a life of
love, dependent on the Father, is the example I look to.
There is nothing that you did without the Father, and I have
that same access. You have given me everything I need
in the Spirit. I have every tool to live a life of surrender
while reflecting the values of your kingdom. I am forever
indebted to you, and gladly so. I have done nothing to
deserve the kind of grace you continually give, yet here I
am living in it. Thank you.

*Are you confident that God's grace
covers all your weaknesses?*

Redemption

"As for you, you meant evil against me; but God meant it for good, in order to bring it about as it is this day, to save many people alive."

GENESIS 50:20 NKJV

Redeemer, you are rich in love to all. You are the master restorer, who takes broken things and makes them new again. You do not fix with tape and glue, temporarily putting things back together. You use the best materials and replace the broken parts with brand new ones. You don't treat us, or our broken lives, haphazardly. You take incredible care in your work of healing and restoration. I ask that you fill me with that same attention to detail. I want to bring my whole heart to the table in what I do and especially to my relationships.

When I serve, let me do it with a heart of compassion. I don't want my obedience to your law of love to become superficial or hasty, more about appeasing my own ego than it is about others knowing your great mercy for them. Your way is always better, and I want to reflect you well, not like a smudged window. You take the worst situations and somehow use them to bring benefit to our lives. You're so wonderful.

How have you seen God's redemption in terrible situations?

I Have Faith

Faith is confidence in what we hope for and assurance about what we do not see.

HEBREWS 11:1 NIV

Constant One, you are beautiful in your faithfulness. Though my natural eyes have not seen you, my eyes of faith have recognized evidence of you everywhere I've been. Your character is sown throughout the earth. In every kind gesture, mercy extended rather than judgment crushing others, and the infectious laugh of an innocent child, I see glimpses of you! You still move in power, confounding doctors with your miraculous healing touch. You restore relationships that were beyond repair, with forgiveness and grace as hallmarks of your involvement. You calm the raging of storms, making meteorologists scratch their heads with wonder.

There is no miracle that doesn't point to your loving connection to your people. You are just that good. Every evidence builds my confidence in that which has yet to be fulfilled. I am sure that you are coming again, and you will be revealed as better than any of us could have ever imagined.

What builds your confidence in God?

Goodness Itself

Let love be genuine. Abhor what is evil;
hold fast to what is good.

ROMANS 12:9 ESV

Good Father, everything you are is full of life. The passion of your heart pours itself out over us with unending goodness and favor. Your love covers every lack of our character; you delight in restoring us to you not because of what we lack, but because of who you are. It is almost too much to comprehend. Without your revelation, there is no chance for understanding. Though we see in part, we will one day fully know even as we are fully known. What a hope!

Lord, let my life be drenched in the oil of your love, soaking into every dry and cracked part until every cell is saturated in you. It is not too much to ask of you when you willingly offer your love to all. I am undone by your affection. Under the weight of it, I am coming alive. I feel like my heart could burst with love. Let me live in this place, making it easy to hold fast to your goodness and reject everything that distorts it.

Are you loving out of an abundance of the love God gives, or giving it away, hoping you'll receive something in return?

Willing to Listen

A wise warning to someone who will listen
is as valuable as gold earrings or fine gold jewelry.

PROVERBS 25:12 NCV

Wonderful Counselor, in you is all wisdom. You are the source of every good piece of advice. Wisdom doesn't offer easy outs though it is always the best way. Your Word says that we should seek wisdom more than gold or silver. Lord, you see my open heart that wants your wise input on every important matter in life. Help me to listen. When you see my heart growing hardened to choose what is imprudent, would you lovingly give me the bigger picture to snap me out of it? I know that you give me freedom to choose, and I'm so thankful for that liberty.

As my advisor, I give you permission to get real with me when I need it. Sometimes I will need a reality-check, and other times, an encouragement to boldly walk in faith. Thank you for wisdom that isn't one-size-fits-all; you're so much better than that. Let me always value your input above any of my own inclinations. And let me be a vessel of your insight, looking out for the best interest of others. Be glorified in the choices I make.

Are you willing to listen to a wise friend's warning?

Better than Life

Because Your lovingkindness is better than life,
My lips will praise You.

PSALM 63:3 NASB

Great God, your love is better than life. It is more precious to me than my most prized treasure. It is more essential to my well-being than a good night's sleep. Your love is more necessary than the food that gives me energy for my day. It is more refreshing than the water that hydrates and sustains life. It is beyond comprehension, not able to be measured. It is the source of all the strength I'll ever need.

It pushes out every fear, covers every weakness, and pulls out the impurities that hide deep under the surface. It is everything you are, and somehow more. Or maybe that's the essence of who you are—more than we can imagine. Incomprehensible abundance. I am in awe of you. What else can I say? You've blown me away with your goodness again, and all I can do is worship you.

How has God's love surprised you?

Without Regret

Godly grief produces a repentance that leads to salvation and brings no regret, but worldly grief produces death.

2 CORINTHIANS 7:10 NRSV

Merciful Father, you are abundant in forgiveness, never turning away from those who come to you with humble hearts. Your love never misses the mark. Your kindness leads me to repentance. When I see the bigger picture—the effects of my sin on others and myself—the grief that leads me to your feet is almost unbearable. But there you meet me with the abundance of your merciful love that covers every failure. Your mercy turns my wounded soul into a new creation, full of the joy of reconciliation! There is no regret in aligning my heart to your great love.

Even in grief, there is renewal. But the grief of the world has no hope; it is a black hole of pain without lasting solutions. What a relief that I am yours, that I know your love and am found in you. I have a hope. Thank you, Lord!

How has forgiveness shaped the way you deal with pain in your life?

No More Boulders

"Build up, build up, prepare the road!
Remove the obstacles out of the way of my people."

ISAIAH 57:14 NIV

Mighty God, in you is power to move every mountain. You prepare a path for your people, and we walk in your way. Lord, when the obstacles of life appear, will you make a way through? Remove the boulders and lead me on. I will trust you each step of this journey of life; I will not take your presence for granted. You are the best leader, and I'm grateful to follow you anywhere. Keep me close when the path gets narrow and there are drop-offs on either side.

I trust that you know my every need; I press into you. Keep me safe and give me the boldness I need to step out in faith when a mountain needs to be moved. I want to grow in confidence with you, Father, following your prompting when it's time to test out new abilities and gifts. Whatever I do, I know you are right here to help fill in for my lack.

*What obstacles have kept you
stuck in one place for too long?*

Seize My Heart

Let us pursue the things which make for peace
and the things by which one may edify another.

ROMANS 14:19 NKJV

Adonai, you are the holy one. You move and I am
awestruck. You fill me with wonder every time. God of
mercy, you freely give away your love to all who would
receive it. Let my heart always stay aware of the richness
of your love, letting it change me in every stage of my life.
There is no one like you; you love me to life time and again.
I want to look like you. You build pathways of peace and
entryways of encouragement. Let my life reflect you; may I
be a peace-bringer and mercy-slinger.

Let my words reflect the grace and love which you so
willingly lavish on your people. There isn't another who so
freely gives out of abundance. I don't know anyone who
generously gives away the best of their house continually
and never runs out. Let me live with the knowledge that I
can always offer mercy, peace, grace, love, and joy because
there is an endless supply available to me. Your resources
don't dry up and they don't run out. I won't hold back.

What has your heart been pursuing?

Too Much

> "Come to me, all who labor and are heavy laden,
> and I will give you rest."
>
> MATTHEW 11:28 ESV

Constant One, you are the one who I depend on in every season and situation. You hold me together when I am falling apart under the weight of the anxieties of this world. When I am heartbroken, you rebuild my heart. Somehow I find that it has a greater capacity in the end. Where there was deep pain, there is now an even deeper measure of love. When crises in life cut me down to size, you build me up. I find I am strengthened by the humility and deep joy that results from embracing the process of grief.

When profound loss wiped me out, I found rest in your comforting arms. It's where I still turn. Even when I couldn't sense you, I knew that you were with me. In the light of day, I see your steady presence more clearly than I ever could have in the darkest night. I am so grateful that you brought me through; I thought I was lost in endless darkness. Thank you for never giving up on me. I won't give up on you now.

When the weight of life is too much, where do you turn?

Self-Discipline

*Since we are approaching the end of all things,
be intentional, purposeful, and self-controlled
so that you can be given to prayer.*

1 PETER 4:7 TPT

God of power, you are my strength. You have everything
I need to face any situation. When I come up against
temptations that promote my own comfort and do nothing
to benefit anyone, may I be rooted in your grace. I know
your grace empowers me in every situation. With your
help, I can assert self-control. I am quick to rave about the
nice-sounding fruit of the Spirit, but self-control is often
left out. However, when I practice it, the intentionality feels
like freedom.

I'm so grateful for your wisdom that pushes me outside
of my comfort zone and leads me into greater freedom in
you. Your ways are better than my own; I submit myself to
you again, knowing that what you require is for my benefit.
Let my life be full of intention and purpose. You are my
great reward and worth every sacrifice I could ever bring.

How does self-discipline make space in your life?

Accountability

As iron sharpens iron,
so a friend sharpens a friend.

PROVERBS 27:17 NLT

Faithful One, your continual stream of grace in my life is the source where I find strength. When I am in need, I turn to you. Your friendship is the strongest relationship in my life; you're so reliable! God, you fill every need with your love. There is nothing I lack that you don't have abundance to meet it. In my friendships, I taste your goodness.

We were not created to live isolated or alone; how grateful I am for that. In relationships, where we're rubbing up against each other's rough edges, how we are tested to love, forgive, and extend mercy! We are sharpened by each other's wise insights, by the comfort we give and the understanding of someone who walks through the trenches with us. What beauty! Thank you for community even in the hard and tense seasons. You are good, wise, and true. These qualities I see in my friendships too.

Who keeps you accountable?

Take Courage

He said, "Come." And when Peter had come down out
of the boat, he walked on the water to go to Jesus.

MATTHEW 14:29 NKJV

Faithful One, you are consistent in your pursuit. How I
became the object of your affection is a mystery—one
that blows my mind. How the God of all creation chose me
as his own before the foundations of the earth astounds
me. You call me by name, knowing every detail about me.
When you call for me to come, how could I let the safety
of my comfort zone hold me back from meeting you? Your
faith in me gives me the courage I need to step out into the
unknown and meet you in the middle of it.

Your love is more than I could have hoped for; it will
forever be beyond my understanding. But a life lived with
the potter who formed my heart as my guide is better than
any I could ever forge on my own. Your love is better than
my wildest dreams. I will live out my thanks to you, giving
you praise with every breath.

*What is holding you back from stepping out
where God is calling you?*

No Despair

The righteous person may have many troubles,
but the LORD delivers him from them all.

PSALM 34:19 NIV

God my hope, you are my deliverer. You save me from
every trouble, meeting me with your abundant grace that
strengthens me. You are all that I need and more. You
didn't promise me a trouble-free life as I follow you; I lay
down all expectations of an easy, comfortable life. What
you did vow was that you will always be with me: an ever-
present help in time of trouble. Your presence carries me
through the darkest nights; it is the comfort that brings me
peace. Your presence gives me the courage I need to keep
going when I want to give up.

I will not fear what tomorrow may bring, knowing your
constant love is with me in every moment. There is not a
millisecond that I am left alone. I don't carry my burdens
alone, and I never have to. Thank you, Lord, for the relief
you bring. I am so grateful.

What trouble do you need deliverance from?

Beyond Reason

What should we say about this?
If God is for us, no one can defeat us.

ROMANS 8:31 NCV

Defender, you are the support I lean on in my weakness. You are my advocate, fighting for me. I will not be afraid of the situations that threaten to take me out; I am tethered to your love, and your love is stronger than death! If you've got a hold of me, nothing can steal my peace. I will not worry, knowing that you are better than the life I live. You are worth everything I could ever sacrifice, including all my comfort. I know that you hold me in the center of your affection. I am held by your grace.

With you by my side, I can't lose. What can be taken away is not worth the life I find in you. You are my holy hope, Lord, and I take courage in you. I lay all my fears before you and invite your perfect love to drive out every single one. Thank you for calling me yours!

Do you believe that God is for you?

Surrendered

Instead, you ought to say, "If the Lord wills,
we will live and also do this or that."

JAMES 4:15 NCV

Holy One, while I am limited in my scope of understanding,
your wisdom spans the ages. You don't have any
limitations. As one who is very aware of my shortcomings,
I'm so relieved to be covered by, and connected to, a
perfect God. My confidence doesn't lie in my own abilities,
but in your faithful goodness toward me. As I make plans
for the future, I willingly surrender them to you, knowing
you always know what's best! I will not hold so tightly
to my dreams – even the ones that you have given me
– that I'm not willing to be redirected by the one who
passionately pursues my heart.

Lord, when you ask for surrender, you're not putting
me into handcuffs. Rather, you are making room for me
to receive from you in a new way. Let me never be so
preoccupied with my plans that I forget that you are after
my heart: to make it whole in you. I offer everything that
keeps me in cycles of brokenness on your altar of mercy.
Make me whole.

*If God were to change the direction of your future,
how would you react?*

Lean in Closer

He gives more grace. Therefore it says, "God opposes the proud, but gives grace to the humble."

JAMES 4:6 ESV

Lord of my heart, I lean into you today. You meet me with the abundance of your mercy that is new every morning. You know exactly how I'm feeling right at this moment. You see the state I'm in; it's not a mystery to you. Thank you for your generous grace that perfectly meets me where I'm at but doesn't leave me unchanged. Your strength becomes my own as I lean on your support. You hold me up when I would otherwise fall.

Lord, would you breathe fresh hope into me today? I don't get it from wishful thinking or from weighing the facts; it only comes from you. Who can extinguish the light that you shine? As I rest in you today, I know you will give me all that I need. Fill me with your glorious life that renews me from the inside out. What you give, no one can take away.

What do you need more of from the Lord today?

November

Be faithful to pray
as intercessors who
are fully alert and
giving thanks to God.

Colossians 4:2 tpt

There Is Hope

"You will have confidence, because there is hope;
you will be protected and take your rest in safety."

JOB 11:18 NRSV

Yahweh, you are the firm foundation that I stand upon.
Your love is always pouring out, but at the same time it
provides the strongest base. When I stand on it, I cannot
be moved. I will rejoice in hope, confident in your ability
to carry out whatever you have set in your heart to
accomplish. My security is found in you; I don't trust the
systems or people of this world to save me. I certainly
know that I'm not up to the task.

Where everyone else falls short, you have abundance to
meet every need. There is no situation too big for you, no
enemy that could intimidate you. You stand alone in power
and strength. What a relief that I'm standing with you and
not against you. My assurance is in your faithfulness. I won't
be afraid. When I begin to forget your greatness, I will look
back and remember what you have done. My heart will be
encouraged again as I recount your wonderful ways.

*When your hope is dwindling, where do you
turn for encouragement?*

Pray for Others

Confess your sins to each other and pray for each other so that you may be healed. The earnest prayer of a righteous person has great power and produces wonderful results.

JAMES 5:16 NLT

Wonderful God, in your wisdom you set us in families and communities. You knew that we needed each other; family was your design from the outset of creation. You wanted us to share our lives with each other. I'm so thankful that I was never meant to be alone. I am not a self-sufficient island. When life gets to be too much to bear, help me to reach out to those around me for help.

Help me to pray consistently for the people in my life. I know my faith will be strengthened as much as theirs will be in answers to prayer. I have seen your power at work in my village of friends, and it leaves me wanting more. Build me up as I live within the context of community, sharing in both the victories and the burdens that we walk through. I will know you more as I live with the grace given in relationship.

When is the last time you prayed with a friend?

Until I Do

Certainly God has heard me;
He has attended to the voice of my prayer.

PSALM 66:19 NKJV

God my shield, you keep me secure in the safety of your arms. I won't be afraid because you are with me. Your faithful love covers me in my present and momentary troubles. I know that you hear me. You won't ignore me or let me waste away. Even as I cry out for you, I realize that I am already inside of your embrace.

There is nothing that can separate me from you. You will answer me; I am strengthened with the support of your arms holding me. I am fully covered, from head to toe, with the kindness of your mercy that has called me your own. I bear your signature; no one can erase it. It is written into my DNA. I am so incredibly thankful for you, and that I am found in you. May I remain firmly fastened to you all the days of my life.

When was the last time God answered one of your prayers?

Not Alone

The Lord God said, "It is not good for the man
to be alone. I will make a helper suitable for him."

GENESIS 2:18 NIV

Creator, you were so full of intention in everything you formed. You took your time in creativity, making everything from the sun to the fish in the sea. Your breath brought flesh and bones to life. Making man in your image, you knew that isolation wasn't the way; relationship would always be the context for the meaning of life. Thank you for setting us in connection with each other and with you from the start. Heal the broken mindsets of your people that say that isolation and independence are preferable. Your way is not easy, but it is always the better way.

Help me to choose the way of love that lays down its own inclinations in favor of the power only experienced in connection with others. I want to choose to show up, not just physically, but emotionally, as well, putting to death the idea that my attention doesn't matter. Give me perspective when I need it. You always know what you're doing, and I submit to you.

Do you depend on yourself more than others?

Golden Rule

"Do to others what you want them to do to you.
This is the meaning of the law of Moses
and the teaching of the prophets."

MATTHEW 7:12 NCV

Merciful God, you never withhold your compassion from those who need it. Your kindness never runs out, and your love is an endless supply. May I never swerve from the golden rule that says to treat others the way I would want to be treated. Reciting this seems so flat; I don't want your truth to become stale.

I will freely extend mercy to others, confident that I need it myself on a regular basis. I will forgive quickly, not wanting any grudges held against me. I will give people the benefit of the doubt, hoping others will have the same courtesy. I will be honest and direct with my needs and expectations, in love, knowing that is how I would want to be communicated with. In all I do, let me honor others as I would like to be honored. May the revelation of your love intensify this desire within me.

*Are your attitudes and actions consistent
with how you expect to be treated by others?*

Let Love Rule

Beyond all these things put on love,
which is the perfect bond of unity.

COLOSSIANS 3:14 NASB

Abba, perfect love comes straight from you. There is nothing that your affection doesn't touch. I can't escape it. The law of your loyal love is the ultimate principle to live by, yet it is so much more than an idea. It is tangible; it is blood poured out, body crucified, buried, and finally, resurrected. Your love is the driving force of the universe. Your pure kindness and affection is what holds us all together.

May I never grow so accustomed to your kindheartedness that I take it for granted and shrug with carelessness at those who just don't get it. As I have been transformed by your compassion, may I take it on, letting it become my motivation to pour it out freely to others, unwilling to keep the best gift I've ever received to myself. Your incredible love is too good to hoard; the very nature of it is generous. Who am I to try to mold it into something else for my own comfort? Let me be a vessel of your love that pours out as freely as it pours in.

How freely does love flow from your life?

I Am yours

"I have not come to call the righteous
but sinners to repentance."

LUKE 5:32 ESV

Holy One, you are worthy of everything I could ever offer.
You already have my life; it is submitted to you. You have
access to every part, King of my heart. You hold my future,
my past is marked by your love, and your Spirit empowers
me in the present. My mind is yielded to you. Write the
words of life in my thoughts. I don't forget where I started
or where I came from. You came into my tumultuous life
and brought peace to the chaos. I am overcome with
emotion thinking about your mercy over my life.

You have been so faithful to me. I know that you won't stop
now. Your goodness is deposited all over my story; thank you
that it's still being written. I trust that when I look back at
the end of my life, the mark of your mercy will be clear, even
clearer than it's been. You are the most talented of story
weavers. I can hardly wait to see where this all ends up. I
know your faithfulness will be laced through the whole thing.

*How does it make you feel when you consider God
is writing your story as you submit to him?*

Greater Good

We know love by this, that he laid down his life for us—
and we ought to lay down our lives for one another.

1 JOHN 3:16 NRSV

Savior, your love outdoes every other with no competition.
You put aside your throne in a perfect kingdom and limited
yourself to human frailty. You displayed for me the perfect
love of the Father that would go to any lengths to restore
broken connection. In laying down your life for me to find my
freedom, you called me to lay down my life in love, displaying
the lengths you still go. Lord, what a reminder that brute
force and intimidation does nothing for lasting peace.

Restoration happens in the laying down, not in the puffing
up. May I stay here, knitted into the love that breaks chains
and calms every storm. The love that walks the path of
peace is not a popular road, but I will take it following you.
Your wisdom offends the wisdom of this world, yet it is the
higher way that always finds lasting solutions sown in love.
I want to be found on your side at every juncture of my life.
Keep me close, Lord, as I choose you.

How can you choose love today?

What If

"Don't be concerned about what to eat and what to drink. Don't worry about such things."

LUKE 12:29 NLT

Rock of Ages, you are the boulder that cannot be moved. Who can crack the foundation of your love? Who can be shaken when they stand on you? All the resources are yours; in you, there is no lack. God, as I look at the areas of my life that are begging for your provision, I will not be moved by worry. I know that you have more than enough. Let your grace flow into the pathways of my mind, leading to peaceful thoughts that rest in your faithfulness.

I won't be afraid when I consider your tangible goodness. I have seen you come through many times in countless ways. Your character hasn't changed since then. Calm the stirring of anxiety that wreaks havoc on my nervous system. Keep me steadily trusting in you. My confidence is in you, the maker of heaven and earth. I don't rely on my own charm or wit to get me by; you are my advocate and my defender. I trust in you.

What worries can you hand over to the Lord today?

Just Decide

Remember to stay alert and hold firmly to all
that you believe. Be mighty and full of courage.

1 CORINTHIANS 16:13 TPT

Father, you are the light that shines in the darkness. When
I can't see what's right in front of my face, I press into you
and trust the light of your countenance will light the path
before me. I will not forget where I came from. You picked
me up from the dust and shook me off, clothing me in your
righteousness.

You made me new, and you never stopped. Your love is
still transforming me. Give me the courage I need to keep
running the race set before me. I know when I cross the
finish line, I'll have reached your kingdom. In the meantime,
you deposit gifts out of your perfect character in my
path, giving me everything I need to keep going. Your
faithfulness leads me on with every breath and every step.
You are pure goodness. I won't let go of you, for you never
let go of me.

What belief about God keeps you going
when you would have given up?

Life of Blessings

"By the God of your father who will help you,
by the Almighty who will bless you
with blessings of heaven above."

GENESIS 49:25 ESV

Faithful Father, you are the giver of all good things. It is no mystery that you are the best gift giver. You know all and love to pour out blessings on your people. Your gifts reflect the generosity of your heart. When I am tempted to think that I am missing out on various things, direct my eyes to the blessings that you have sown within my life. Look at all that you have given me. How could I be disappointed when you have been so liberal with your love?

I see you, Lord. I see where you have hidden treasures for me to find in my lineage. There is beauty in connecting the generations, even those that, at first glance, don't seem to draw a straight line. Your love is woven through; the threads are visible at certain points and hidden at others. But the strand running through it is unmistakable. Thank you for blessing that reaches beyond my life, Father.

What blessings are you enjoying because of choices
that previous generations made?

you Remain

Jesus Christ is the same yesterday and today
and forever.

HEBREWS 13:8 NASB

Steadfast God, you are unchanging. What a comfort and
a joy, to know that you remain constant through the ages.
Jesus, your character has never wavered in its purpose
to reflect the Father's loyal love to all who would pay
attention. I am so grateful for kindness that is unable to
be dissuaded. Your goodness won't ever let up. You have
not all of a sudden become stingy with grace. Your mercy
remains free for all who would receive.

Lord, I won't stop aligning myself to you. You are the most
beautiful person I've ever known. I won't ever meet anyone
who outshines you. Today, would you root me deeper in
the constancy of your great affection over my life? Your
love transforms me into the person you always intended
me to be. I am in the process of becoming. You are my
faithful companion, and I am yours forever. When all else
passes away, you remain unchanged.

How does God's constancy fuel your faith?

Let Them Choose

When the people of Israel heard about King Solomon's decision, they respected him very much. They saw he had wisdom from God to make the right decisions.

1 KINGS 3:28 NCV

God, you are the ultimate freedom fighter. You don't rule like a dictator, demanding respect and holding onto your power through manipulation and fear tactics. You are the most benevolent king! You freely give away the bounty of your resources to all who ask. When we come to you, you open your home and throw a great banquet, laying out a feast. Even if it's just a few who show up, it does not affect the level of your response. You are ever-welcoming, always generous with joy. You are beyond good, Father.

May everyone hear and know of your everlasting goodness. Your kingdom has open borders that welcomes strangers in the same way it does family. Let everyone have the same chance to choose. Who would turn down such an invitation? Lord, fill me with your revelation that brings your Word alive. You are so good, God – I choose you, Lord, and I choose to eat of the wisdom of your bountiful kingdom!

How do you make major decisions in your life?

Out of Hiding

Whoever conceals his transgressions will not prosper,
but he who confesses and forsakes them
will obtain mercy.

PROVERBS 28:13 ESV

Holy One, you cover every one of my sins with the mercy that flows freely from your throne. I don't hide myself from you; you see everything done in secret. I need the power of your love to cover me with your love and to lift me out of the spiral of shame. You are better than I expect every time. In humility, I offer every part of me for your inspection. Your mercy has free access to my heart. Your light shines, and I find that I am seized by your affection; you don't hesitate. Your love knocks out every fear, and the reluctance that I had disappears!

Thank you for mercy that meets me when my experience with others has me expecting disappointment and guilt-trips. You lift every weight and my heaviness is traded for joy that sets my feet dancing. I can't help but rejoice, Lord. You're always better to me than I anticipate.

What is keeping your from coming to the Lord with all that you are?

Family Matters

If someone does not know how to manage his own household, how can he take care of God's church?

1 TIMOTHY 3:5 NRSV

Father, you lead us freely with the wisdom you have. There are no mysteries to you, and you're not searching for answers. I come to you today with an open heart ready to receive your grace. There is nothing I have need of that you can't supply; I just know it. You are the anchor that keeps me from drifting when storms of confusion come to toss me around. You are the cleft I hide in when the arrows of the enemy are threatening me. You set me on the rock, your firm foundation, and no matter what, your bedrock doesn't crack or shift.

Lord, I hear your heart when you examine my life and challenge my ways. If I am faithful with what I have, it reflects in you; if I don't show care to my own, then how could I ever care for those who don't belong to me? Give me grace to give myself fully to my family; they are not a lesser priority in your kingdom. Your love starts first there. I hear you, Lord, and I repent for how I've neglected love for my own gain or comfort. Bring restoration.

Do you put your family first over your ministry or job?

Celebrate Perfection

"Why do you call me good?" Jesus asked.
"Only God is truly good."

MARK 10:18 NLT

Perfect One, in you everything finds their fulfillment. God over all, you keep pouring yourself out in goodness to all who come to you. There is not a day where you're running low on loyal love; you don't wake up on the wrong side of the bed. You always keep a watchful, loving eye, and your moods don't shift with the weather. Your ways are higher and your heart is truer. Whatever I could hope to find in your hand is nothing compared to what I find in your heart of compassion. All lovingkindness flows from that place; I find I'm drenched in it when I spend time in your presence.

I celebrate your goodness, Lord! I could go on about how beautiful you are, but right now I give myself to your presence, letting you sweep over me again. I set my mind on you- meet me here and transform me again by your grace.

How does God's goodness fill your life?

Friend of God

One who has unreliable friends soon comes to ruin,
but there is a friend who sticks closer than a brother.

PROVERBS 18:24 NIV

Good Shepherd, you lead me through every mountain and valley of this life. It is your voice I follow. As I walk with you as my guide, I will not falter or fail. Though I may stumble, you will catch me. Though traps are laid out, you will rescue me if I get caught. You are the most faithful friend I've ever known. You are with me in the long, dark valleys and you are with me on the mountaintop. You share with me in every celebration and every devastation; you grieve with me in my sorrow.

You are closer to me than my own flesh and blood. Though they love me as they are able, your love is perfect, washing away the pain of misunderstanding and unmet expectations from every other relationship. Where I have learned to relate to you in faulty ways, tear down and rebuild the connection. I know that you will never fail me, God. Don't let me forget the wonder and security of this pure love.

Do you trust God's friendship to stick with you through thick and thin?

Thank you

Let us be thankful, because we have a kingdom that cannot be shaken. We should worship God in a way that pleases him with respect and fear.

HEBREWS 12:28 NCV

Holy God, the heavens declare your glory by their very existence. Every eye sees their beauty; who could miss it? Yet, even if it could be overlooked, your kingdom remains truer. It is set on the bedrock of your unfailing love; nothing can shake or destroy it. Thank you for a kingdom that lasts. There has been no other in all of history that has maintained its power through the ages. You, though, don't rule in fear or intimidation. You reign in honor and with mercy freely flowing to all who seek refuge in you.

I worship you, Lord, for you are nobler than the most honorable ruler. You are truer than the most loyal friend. You are beyond comprehension and yet the fulfillment of knowledge. I am undone at the thought that I am yours. Thank you; may I follow in your ways and customs all the days of my life, until your kingdom can be seen with the naked eye and all are amazed by the beauty of your majesty. You will be seen in all your fullness and glory!

What about God's kingdom are you thankful for?

Always Hope

The prayer of faith will save the sick,
and the Lord will raise him up.
And if he has committed sins, he will be forgiven.

JAMES 5:15 NKJV

Lord, fill my heart afresh with the liquid love of your presence. Fill me to overflowing. I receive all that you offer, knowing that you are the supply I reach from throughout my day. The more I have, the more there is to give. Lord, you are the hope of my heart—of every longing, dream, and desire. You have not forgotten the promises you have spoken. You won't go back on your Word.

My soul is encouraged when I look over my life and see how you have shown up at every stage. What a wonderful tapestry of love and redemption you are weaving. Even now, I can feel my faith being strengthened as I remember what you have already done. I see your faithfulness, Lord. It is undeniable. Do it again, Lord – heal the sick, mend the broken, and raise the dead. Your ways are impossibly good!

When you consider God's goodness at work in your life, how does that make you think about the future?

Deserved Thanks

Let every activity of your lives and every word that comes from your lips be drenched with the beauty of our Lord Jesus, the Anointed One. And bring your constant praise to God the Father because of what Christ has done for you!

COLOSSIANS 3:17 TPT

Father, I come to you with a heart full of gratitude today. When I list the ways you have faithfully showed up time and again in my life with your consistent love, I am overwhelmed! God, may everything I do, every word that comes out of my mouth, point people to your faithfulness. Your goodness is beyond what I could begin to describe, but I'll try. Your kindness always leads me back to you when I have started to drift off course. You have never let go of me or let me down even when I was sure that you had disappointed me, you gave me a perspective that showed your incredible love in a new way.

There is no one like you. You are perfect in how you care for me, knowing exactly what I need when I need it. You never let jealousy overtake your senses; you are patient in love. I could go on forever, and in eternity, I will. For now, let the overflow of gratitude in my heart be enough.

How can you thank God for his goodness today?

What Better Gift

The Spirit of the LORD will rest on Him,
The spirit of wisdom and understanding,
The spirit of counsel and strength,
The spirit of knowledge and the fear of the LORD.

ISAIAH 11:2 NASB

Ever-present One, I can't begin to tell you how thankful I am that your Spirit is in me. The constant presence that brings comfort when no one else even knows that my heart is grieved feels too good to be true. The wisdom I am searching for is found in the one who is already dwelling with me. Every tool I need to know the Lord, and every act on God's part in my life, is done through fellowship with the Spirit.

You are the light inside of me. Any compassion I have or look for is found in you. A million thank-yous for the way you are consistently with me would not even scratch the surface of my true debt of gratitude. I am so grateful I get to do life with you. You are the best gift I could not even imagine to ask for; what beauty is found in companionship with you.

How does walking with the Spirit enrich your life?

In Kindness

"You gave me life and showed me kindness,
and in your providence watched over my spirit."

JOB 10:12 NIV

Wonderful Counselor, it is your kindness that leads me back to you again and again. Your wonderful way of mercy, saturated in lovingkindness, is the path of life that brings light to every shadow of a doubt that blows in. You teach with words covered in your trademark love even in correction. You have kept an eye on me my whole life, even when I was off chasing my own dark desires. You kept me from the grip of death. You lured me in with your persuasively persistent love that seemed too good to be true. It still does!

Thank you for your gentleness that tenderly cares for the vulnerable heart. You don't despise me in my weakness – you offer your own strength. You cover the distance between my heart and yours with a single step. You are never far away, and of that I am grateful. Lord, may I show the same kindness to others as you continually offer me.

How does kindness change your perception of someone?

Humility of Jesus

He poured water into the basin, and began to wash the disciples' feet and to wipe them with the towel with which He was girded.

JOHN 13:5 NASB

Humble God, you are the ultimate servant. What an upside-down reality. The King of kings became the servant of all. I can't understand it. Why would you leave the glory of your dwelling place, where you were fully honored and revered, to take on the fleshly form of a boy living in relative obscurity? I know it's your love that drove you. Give me revelation to comprehend the incredible implications of your sacrifice. You didn't lord your authority over your disciples or require that they do anything that you, yourself, wouldn't do. In your living, you taught them to live.

May I follow your example, Jesus, humbly serving others in the name of love. Even the least-appealing act of service is meaningful when I do it with the intention of honoring people. Your approach is better than my own. Let me be more like you.

How can you humbly serve someone today?

Have Mercy

Let us therefore approach the throne of grace with
boldness, so that we may receive mercy and
find grace to help in time of need.

HEBREWS 4:16 NRSV

Gracious God, in my time of need, I come to you. I follow
the call of your heart of love that beckons me deeper into
your presence. Here I find everything I need. There is mercy
to meet me in the reality where I am; there is grace to
cover every weakness. There is strength to fuel my feeble
efforts and peace that calms all anxiety. Anything I could
ever ask for is found here in your presence. Thank you,
God, that I get to come freely to you. I get to approach
your throne of grace with the boldness that comes from
being your child.

Lord, as I confidently come before you, knowing that I will
receive the help I need whenever I ask, let me be filled to
overflowing with grace that I freely give to others as I have
received. May I pour out mercy in the same measure that I
have been given. The abundance of your kingdom knows
no limits.

Do you have mercy to give to others?

Made New

Create in me a clean heart, O God,
and put a new and right spirit within me.

PSALM 51:10 NRSV

God of my renewal, everything you touch becomes filled
with your invigorating life. You breathe into barren places
and cause fruitful vines to grow. Your resurrection power
makes the impossible a reality, and I have confident
assurance in this same power at work in my life. When I
thought I was lost, without a trace of hope holding me
together, you showed up with your faithful hand of mercy
to save me. How could I begin to thank you? When I
think about my life before I really knew you, it is nearly
impossible to imagine where I'd be now if you hadn't
intervened.

Lord, today I ask for you to touch my heart again. What has
grown cold, melt with the passion of your heart. I am yours.
Take what is no longer useful—the dead parts of me—and
change them with your mercy that makes me new.

What needs the renewing touch of the Spirit in your life?

Miracle Enough

"Will you never believe in me unless you see miraculous signs and wonders?"

JOHN 4:48 NLT

Yahweh, in you everything finds its rightful place. As I approach your throne of grace today, I ask for your Holy Spirit to surround me. Fill me with the satisfaction that only comes from knowing you. Thank you for moving in powerful ways around the earth and in my own life. May my faith not be established in answered prayers; may it find its confidence in you. You say that prophecies will cease and knowledge will be dismissed, but your love—your primary character trait—will never come to an end.

I believe in you because of your love, Lord. It is what drew me in the first place. Every day of my life, I am drinking its life-giving waters. When I start to make demands of you based on my own desires, let me remember that knowing you is the greatest gift of all.

What fuels your belief in God?

A Way Home

All things are of God, who has reconciled us to Himself
through Jesus Christ, and has given us the ministry
of reconciliation.

2 CORINTHIANS 5:18 NKJV

Restorer, you have done the hard work of redemption. In
you all things were created, and in you all things find their
healing. God of grace, you did not leave us to wander this
earth without hope. Through Jesus, we have been reunited
with you. The veil in the holy temple that separated the
people from your tangible presence was torn when Jesus
breathed his last breath. When he broke loose from the
grave three days later, even death was defeated, not
leaving anything in this life or the next to keep us from
being with you!

Thank you, Lord, that I have been reconciled with you,
able to boldly come before your throne of grace anytime. I
come to you confidently today with every care I carry. I will
not take for granted the beauty of this relationship. You are
incredible, and I thank you.

*Do you confidently believe that you can go to God
with anything at any time?*

Not Feeling It

Diligent hands will rule,
but laziness ends in forced labor.

PROVERBS 12:24 NIV

God, when work has made my soul weary and I've grown tired of responsibilities, I ask for your rest to fill my being. I recognize that you rested. It is your example that I follow into the kind of rest that looks like rejuvenation. When I rest and I am tempted to skirt my responsibilities for the comfort of my own whims, I ask for your hand of grace to bring clarity to my mind. You are not a workaholic, so I won't work myself to death, but I also know that you do not set an example of laziness which has no motivation to work at all.

When I lose motivation, remind me what it is I am working for and toward. Where there is vision, there is a goal on the horizon. Refresh my mind when the wind starts going out of my sails. Help me to stay the course and do what is mine to do.

What is your motivation for work?

Waiting for Me

You need to persevere so that when you have done the
will of God, you will receive what he has promised.

HEBREWS 10:36 NIV

Merciful One, give me the grace I need to get through
today. Even as I pray this, I recognize I want more than
just to get through. Whatever lies before me this day will
be met with the sufficiency of your grace. If I face difficult
situations that make me want to run away instead of face
them with kindness and truth, give me the perseverance
I so desperately need. When I want to turn and take the
easy way out instead of choosing the way of your humble
love, fill me with the determination that chooses your way
over my own.

Lord, as I submit my will to yours, I will find life in the end
no matter what the middle ends up looking like. Give me
the strength I need for this day and help me not to get
ahead of myself. I am connected to the source of life; I
believe that I have everything I need for everything I'll face
because I am in you.

When hard situations arise, do you persevere or run away?

First and True

Don't set the affections of your heart on this world or in loving the things of the world. The love of the Father and the love of the world are incompatible.

1 JOHN 2:15 TPT

Lover of my soul, I set my affections on you today. You are the true desire of my heart; in you I find the acceptance and confidence I have been looking for all my life. Keep my heart satisfied in you, that the sway of the world and all its offerings would pale in comparison to the goodness of loving you. Lord, you know my tendency toward complacency, but I don't want that to be a marker of my relationship with you.

I come alive in your river of love; it fills me with joy that can't be found anywhere else. May I stay awake in this age of competing forces for my affection; only you truly satisfy. Everything else comes up empty in the end. I offer you my whole heart—every part—today. I don't hold anything back because you are fully worth all of it.

If you look at the way you spend your time, what are your affections set on?

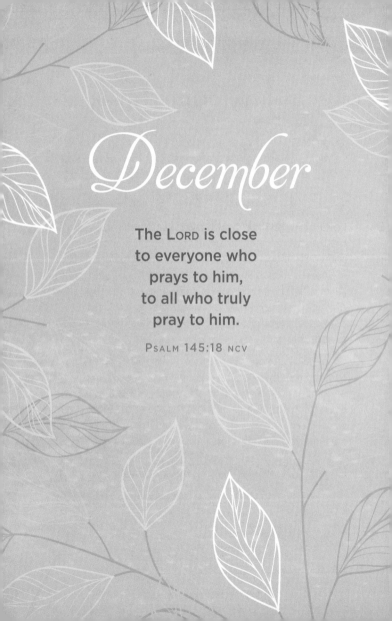

December

The LORD is close
to everyone who
prays to him,
to all who truly
pray to him.

PSALM 145:18 NCV

Make Me Wise

How blessed is the man who finds wisdom
And the man who gains understanding.

PROVERBS 3:13 NASB

Spirit of Wisdom, I know you hold all the answers I've been seeking. My own understanding has taken me as far as it could. My capacity has reached its limit, but you have a limitless supply. Where else would I go in my search of wisdom? If I could buy it, I would have already. But I know that's not how it works. It's better this way because it is based in relationship, and I know you already know every situation I'm asking about.

Lord, speak into my questions; I have so many. Would you give me the direction I long for and peace of mind when I make my informed decisions? Without you, I'll keep wandering around waiting either for signs in the sky or for the time to run up and my decisions will be made for me. Neither of those are good options. Thank you for giving wisdom so willingly. I submit to your leadership and counsel.

What do you need wisdom about?

Ever Brighter

We all, with unveiled face, beholding as in a mirror the glory of the Lord, are being transformed into the same image from glory to glory, just as by the Spirit of the Lord.

2 CORINTHIANS 3:18 NKJV

Great God, as I look to you every day, may I become more and more like you. Your goodness that meets me at every turn of my life is the portion that I feast upon. May my life reflect that goodness to others. You are the light that makes shadows flee and brings clarity to the darkest corners of life. As I spend time in the light of your presence, my life will shine bright for you.

Transform me, God, that I may look like you to the world. Be glorified in my life, even more so as time goes by and I continue to submit my life to you. Let the light of your glory shine on me, and may I come back to you over and over again to soak up your image. As I go from glory to glory in this life, I am being carried by your Spirit which brings light and life wherever it goes. I'm grateful for access to you.

What characteristics are shining bright in your life?

Striving

"Don't work for the food that spoils. Work for the food that stays good always and gives eternal life. The Son of Man will give you this food, because on him God the Father has put his power."

JOHN 6:27 NCV

Good Father, may my heart be set on you as my hands serve others in love. Would you keep me from the trap of self-serving work that only looks out for my own good and benefit? Your love is so much bigger than that, and I know you are taking care of me. Couple wisdom with humility, so I walk in compassion and discernment.

God, you have all that I'm looking for. I don't have to hoard all the things I need. Give me a generous heart that rests in the provision of a good father. As I work for you, keep me from striving that finds no rest and only the desperation of getting it right. I know that as I labor with you, I live in the light of your grace that covers every failure. Shame is not my portion; I am confident in you. As I follow you, I will know your power made evident in my life.

Are you working endlessly for something with an expiration date?

At your Word

It is by faith we understand that the whole world was made by God's command so what we see was made by something that cannot be seen.

HEBREWS 11:3 NCV

Living Word, you are the source and originator of every living thing. Without you, I would not be here—nothing would! When I start to let the darkness of doubt lead me into the black hole of endless unanswered questions, lead me back with the light of your life. You speak, and the mountains tremble. You whisper, and the earth does your bidding.

Great God of the universe, shine the revelation light of your Word into my mind, bringing life to concepts I could not understand without you. I believe that you are the sustainer, as well as the creator. Sustain me with your steady love, keeping me on the path that leads to your kingdom. Fertilize the small seed of faith in my heart with your faithfulness, coming through at every turn. Wherever I go, I see you when I look for you. Give me eyes of faith to see what is to come in you.

Do you believe that God's power still speaks?

Leading Me

Whether you turn to the right or to the left,
your ears will hear a voice behind you, saying,
"This is the way; walk in it."

ISAIAH 30:21 NIV

Leader of my life, I trust that I don't have to conjure up your plans for me. I won't have to struggle to know which way to turn when I come to a fork in the road. As I live intentionally seeking your wisdom and guidance, I know you won't let me down. I take hope in you, knowing you are with me now and in the hour of my need. Your strong hand guides me all the days of my life.

I won't fear the unknown because nothing is unknown to you. What a privilege to walk in the counsel of the all-knowing one. You see every possible outcome, and I trust that as I seek you, you won't lead me into a void. Keep me close to you, always just a whisper away. Your voice fills me with confidence. Keep my ears tuned to you. I rely on you, God.

Do you trust God to lead you?

Free to Serve

As God's loving servants,
you should live in complete freedom,
but never use your freedom as a cover-up for evil.

1 PETER 2:16 TPT

Redeemer, what a wonderful reality that you have set me free with no strings attached. Thank you that you did not purchase my freedom to make me a slave. I get to choose, out of my own heart and will, to follow you. You are so worth it. The goodness that I've tasted and seen in you is only a glimpse of what you have stored up for your people.

Why would I choose to live only for myself and my own good, when that leads to disappointment in the end. Your plans are always better than my own; I've seen that play out too many times to question whether it remains true. Today, I bind my will to yours, not pushing or pulling to get my own way. I trust that your intentions for me and for those around me are better than my own. I will follow where you lead today.

Do you follow God out of the joy of the freedom he gives or out of obligation?

Indescribable Gift

Thanks be to God for his indescribable gift!

2 CORINTHIANS 9:15 NKJV

God, you are the ultimate good gift. You freely pour out your grace, mercy, love, and kindness over your people as we walk this life. All these amazing attributes that attempt to characterize you are but a glimpse into the greatness of who you are. Who can rightfully describe you? Who has seen you with their naked eye? You give me revelations of yourself, but even those fall short. My mind can't comprehend the extent of your goodness.

Jesus, you are the embodiment of God in flesh and bones, poured out. You subjected yourself to man's laws, customs, and limitations, yet I know that you are so much bigger than man's mind can comprehend. I'm just scratching the surface here, right Lord? Lead me into greater understanding of your goodness today. May I see a facet of your character in a new way that I may worship you in awe and wonder.

What is the best gift you've ever received?

No More Sorrow

"He will wipe every tear from their eyes, and there will
be no more death or sorrow or crying or pain.
All these things are gone forever."

REVELATION 21:4 NLT

God of comfort, I know there will come a day when your
kingdom arrives once and for all, and there will be no more
pain. How I long for that day. All sorrow and mourning
will be but a memory, and we will be surrounded by your
perfect love that keeps all fear away. We will forever be
kept in perfect peace. No more wars or rumors of wars; no
more conflict or relational pain. You will make all the wrong
things right and everything will find their fulfillment in the
light of your kingdom. While we wait for that day to arrive,
give us hope in the day to come, knowing this suffering
won't last for eternity.

Fill my heart with courage today. I ask for your comfort
to grab hold of my heart, breathing life and hope into the
very core of my being. Jesus, I believe that you are coming
again; you are returning for your people. May my heart take
courage in you.

Can you imagine a life without sorrow?

Hypocrisy

"You hypocrite! First, take the wood out of your own
eye. Then you will see clearly to take the dust out
of your friend's eye."

MATTHEW 7:5 NCV

God, when I am tempted to judge someone else's actions,
I pray I would be quick to look to my own heart. May the
grace I've received be the grace I freely extend to those
around me. Thank you that I don't have to agree with
others in order to love them well, leaving space for their
own journeys of healing. Keep my heart humble, so when I
have the opportunity to challenge my friends and family, it
would be done with a true heart of love, wanting the best
for them.

When I am blinded by offense, I can offer nothing but my
own indignant opinion. Keep my heart malleable that I
may deal with my own issues by your Spirit. Let love like a
mighty river wash away the subtle lies of the enemy that
fuel the flame of indignation. Keep my heart pure in you.

Are you quick to judge others or to extend grace?

Take Me Deeper

Let us stop going over the basic teachings about Christ
again and again. Let us go on instead and become
mature in our understanding. Surely we don't need
to start again with the fundamental importance of
repenting from evil deeds and placing our faith in God.

HEBREWS 6:1 NLT

Lord my God, you are never changing and yet always
full of new mysteries to discover. I want to know you
more, growing deep in the awareness of who you are, not
simply who I've known you to be. Great God of mercy,
as I learn, may I grow up in you, becoming mature in my
understanding. I don't want to live in the paradigm of
comfort, not willing to go through the growing pains of
development.

May my growth not be stunted by my apathetic
tendencies. Fill me with hunger to search out the deeper
mysteries of your kingdom. All my hope and faith is in
you; as I live out your law of love, bring me the revelation-
knowledge that only those who seek after you find. I want
to dive into deeper waters, not simply stay in the shallow.
Hear my heart and teach me what I have yet to understand.

*Have you become comfortable in your faith,
or is there a hunger for more?*

Not Slow

The Lord is not slow about His promise, as some count slowness, but is patient toward you, not wishing for any to perish but for all to come to repentance.

2 PETER 3:9 NASB

Faithful One, you hold all my days in your loving hand. Your patience keeps you pursuing the hearts of your people when others would have given up. I know that I can lay down my cares before you, trusting in your love to carry out all that you promised. You are not slow in fulfilling your Word; you have not forgotten about it or changed your mind. Your compassionate care for your people outweighs the preferred timeline of mortal minds.

When I start to feel discouragement set in that I have not seen you come through in areas that I've been longing for breakthrough, direct my heart to yours. Give me perseverance to trust that in the death of waiting, there is life ready to spring up in the rightful time. I won't pretend to understand or not be bothered by waiting that tests the limits of my hope, but I will choose to trust you. You never fail. In you, I find the fulfillment of every longing. Take courage, heart of mine, in God who gives strength to every seeking soul.

Have you become discouraged in waiting on God's promise?

Peace on Earth

"Glory to God in the highest,
and on earth peace among those
with whom he is pleased!"

LUKE 2:14 ESV

Prince of Peace, your presence brings life to your people. You are worthy of every offering I could ever give, and more. Words fall short when I consider your indescribable goodness. God of peace, bring calm to the anxieties racing around my head. Bring relief to the tension that has been building in this hectic season. I know that in you, I find the rest I long for.

Today, Lord, meet me in the details of my schedule, giving me quiet confidence to follow through with your presence as my strength. God, you are good. Don't let me forget the beauty of who you are; let the distractions quiet down as I set my heart on you. I invite you into every moment of my day. I belong to you. May all the work I do be from a place of rest in you today.

*What worries and anxieties can you
invite the peace of God into?*

Plan to Please

The plans of the diligent lead surely to plenty,
But those of everyone who is hasty, surely to poverty.

PROVERBS 21:5 NKJV

Lord over all, you are purposeful in everything you do. I want to be like you, intentionally living my life every day for you. Give me vision, that I may see with eyes of love into every situation I walk into. May your faithfulness rub off on me, so I would diligently finish every important task that I start. Let my heart, linked to yours, know that quicker does not mean better; I will patiently do what is mine to do. I will let go of everything else.

Above all, may my character reflect your kindness, goodness, and mercy. May I be full of your light that brings simple solutions to complex problems. Help me to not get distracted by empty promises of things that seem too good to be true. Let me remember that your ways are better than the ways of this world. Your wisdom is my guide; lead me on in your faithful love.

*Have you gotten counsel about
the plans you're working toward?*

Doing My Thing

Each one of us has a body with many parts, and these parts all have different uses. In the same way, we are many, but in Christ we are all one body. Each one is a part of that body, and each part belongs to all the other parts.

ROMANS 12:4-5 NCV

Good Father, I see your goodness in the diversity of your people. Thank you that we were never meant to be cookie-cutter people. I was created uniquely and wonderfully. I know that my makeup is not the same as everyone else around me. What a great reality. You keep things fresh; you create in similarities, but never carbon copies. I am grateful to know that the strengths and gifts you put in me were with a purpose and a plan, and I get to use them for you.

When I start to compare my weaknesses with others' strengths, remind me that we are all different parts of the same body. A pinky was never meant to have the strength of a leg. I will look to you, God, to find the confidence I need. I lean in to hear your words of life that remind me of my true identity—the person you always created me to be. I will freely operate in the gifts I have.

How do your gifts strengthen and serve others?

Harder Tests

Do not be surprised at the fiery ordeal among you, which comes upon you for your testing, as though some strange thing were happening to you; but to the degree that you share the sufferings of Christ, keep on rejoicing, so that also at the revelation of His glory you may rejoice with exultation.

1 PETER 4:12–13 NASB

Merciful One, let my heart stay soft as I offer all that I am as a living sacrifice to you. I set my heart on you, God, where all my delight and joy can be found. When I walk through fire, I will not be burned. When the waters rise, they will not overtake me. Even in suffering, I will not be discouraged because you have not left me on my own to endure in my feeble strength. You renew me, giving wind to sails that cannot move the ship of my life on their own.

Spirit of God, you refresh me as I rejoice in you. I am so grateful for your waters of life that revive my weary heart and give me strength to face another day. Whatever comes, I know that I can face it with your steady love fueling me. Thank you for your persistent presence.

When you face trials, do you believe that God is with you?

Just that Much

Christ proved God's passionate love for us by dying in our place while we were still lost and ungodly!

ROMANS 5:8 TPT

God of love, your passionate pursuit of your people is incredible. There is no stopping you with extravagant love as your driving force. I am so grateful for your grace that completely covers every weakness, failure, and sin in my life. It all comes back to you. Your sacrifice, Jesus, was the pinnacle: the amazing testament of the lengths that you would go to reveal the Father's heart toward me. When I consider that you created this world and everything in it— from distant galaxies to the very dirt that my house is built upon—how can I be anything but astounded at your care for me?

Thank you, God, for always covering the distance between us. When I call on you, there you are. When I look for you, I find you, for you are with me. I don't know how to say it in a way that adequately describes the meaning behind it, so I'll just say it again—thank you!

Do you believe that God's love is greater than your biggest weakness?

Before this Moment

For every matter there is a time and judgment,
Though the misery of man increases greatly.

ECCLESIASTES 8:6 NKJV

God over all, you see the end from the beginning; nothing is hidden from your sight. Every moment is accounted for, each time falling into its rightful place. As time marches on, it seems as if I blink and already months have passed. I don't want to miss what you're doing. I don't want to miss the purpose of each season. I don't want to get caught up in a day that hasn't yet arrived. Keep my heart set on you, my support. You are steady in your intentions, and I can look to you for my cues.

Lord, I trust your faithful ways, no matter the day or time. Here's my heart again; take and fill it with your love that brings peace and life. I will not be discouraged or disappointed in your timing. I will trust that you know what you're doing better than I do. You are trustworthy.

Are you impatient with God's timing in an area of your life?

Slow Down

The wise see danger ahead and avoid it,
but fools keep going and get into trouble.

PROVERBS 27:12 NCV

God, when I am caught up in the crazy pace of this world
that never stops, help me to remember to pause. In rest,
I can reflect. I see things more clearly when I see them
through the lens of your life. When I am tempted to rush
into things, keep me grounded in the wisdom of your Word.
I know that you honor hearts that seek you. Oh, how I long
to know you more! Fill me with the knowledge of your love
that keeps my feet steady and my heart set on you.

Right now, Lord, I set my intentions on you. Fill me with
your power to practice temperance and self-control. I will
follow in your ways, not going off on my own or getting
caught up in the craze of society. You are better than that; I
will walk in the way of your goodness.

Have you been going nonstop,
or are you making room for reflection and rest?

Bold and Yielding

Going a little farther, he fell on the ground and prayed that, if it were possible, the hour might pass from him. And he said, "Abba, Father, all things are possible for you. Remove this cup from me. Yet not what I will, but what you will."

MARK 14:35–36 ESV

Jesus, you are the perfect example of how to approach the Father. In the anguish of your soul, you laid out your heart and desires before the throne of God. Your boldness, coupled with a humble heart, gives me courage to pour out my own heart, just as it is. And yet, I will yield, just as you did, to the will of the Father.

Here is my heart, Lord; I offer you every part. Hear what my desperation says and know that I am joined to you. Your way is the higher way, and I will humble my will to yours. I trust that you are with me in my suffering, just as you are with me in my victories. When I don't understand what you are doing, hold my heart close as I trust in you. You are the keeper of my days. Your will be done in my life.

Have you honestly poured out your heart to the Lord lately?

Conduit of Comfort

That we may be able to comfort those who are in any trouble, with the comfort with which we ourselves are comforted by God.

2 CORINTHIANS 1:4 NKJV

God my comfort, I cannot begin to thank you for your constant presence with me in my pain. When I thought that I was lost in the darkness of the suffering of my soul, you came in with your loving embrace and wrapped me in the presence of your perfect peace. There is no comfort like yours. You fill the cracks of my gaping wounds like a salve that brings peace and healing. God of my own healing and hope, let me reflect your character by being a comforter to those who mourn.

May I bring your peace as I meet those who are suffering in their pain. Your love is big enough to meet every person in the reality of their hurt; it is strong enough to heal the most intense wounds. I cannot turn away from others who are suffering, knowing that you never run from the broken-hearted. You bind them up and hold them together. Let me be the same, Lord, unafraid to give pain space to be met by the overwhelming love of the Father.

Who is hurting around you that you can offer comfort to?

Finishing

> "I know that You can do all things,
> And that no purpose of Yours can be thwarted."
>
> JOB 42:2 NASB

Alpha and Omega, you are the beginning and the end. Every purpose you've ever laid out is fulfilled, and I know you haven't given up on your promises. Pausing in your presence right now, I ask for a fresh revelation of your faithful love that empowers me to stand strong in faith. Keep my heart steady and my eyes fixed on you, the source and perfecter of my faith. Though the mountains give way and the earth shakes, you remain the same powerful God that you have always been. The plans that you have set in motion cannot be thwarted.

God, I cling to you; I rely on your perfect ways that make a path through the desert and wilderness. You see the end from the beginning. No detail is missed by you. I can trust in your unfailing love to guide me and keep me in this life. When I follow you, I am led into the light of life.

What have you been ready to give up on that God can strengthen you to persevere in?

Blessed Words

A time to tear, and a time to sew;
a time to keep silence, and a time to speak.

ECCLESIASTES 3:7 ESV

Gracious God, you know the times and seasons so well. May I lean into your understanding, knowing when to remain silent and when to speak up. There is discernment in your wisdom, and I need it. When I am tempted to say everything I have stored up within me, let me gauge the timing by turning to you and letting the Spirit be the barometer. I know you won't leave me hanging; don't let me be hasty in my speech, and when I do speak, let my words be laced with love.

May the honey of your grace cover what needs to be said so that even in confrontation and correction, it may be received with humility, leading to reconciliation. When I've done all I could and others reject me, let my words bless them still, and not curse. I wait on you, knowing you will give me the discernment I need for today.

Do you pause to consider your words before you say them?

Cannot Lose

In all these things we are more than conquerors through Him who loved us. For I am persuaded that neither death nor life, nor angels nor principalities nor powers, nor things present nor things to come, nor height nor depth, nor any other created thing, shall be able to separate us from the love of God which is in Christ Jesus our Lord.

ROMANS 8:37–39 NKJV

Powerful God, I come to you with my hands open to receive a new dose of your mercy today. Like a waterfall, flow over me with your unending love that gives me life. Flood me with your rivers of grace that empower me to face anything that may come. There is nowhere I can go and nothing I can do that will make your love less accessible.

What a wonderful reality that I am always connected to your kindness. It is the fuel of my own compassion. What could anyone really do to me if they can't take away my access to your incredible affection? You are the prize of my life, and I live for you. Connected to you by your river of mercy, I will not worry about losing myself along the way, for I have found myself coming alive in you.

What situations can you carry the confidence of God's love into today?

Extravagant Love

A child has been born to us; God has given a son to us.
He will be responsible for leading the people.
His name will be Wonderful Counselor, Powerful God,
Father Who Lives Forever, Prince of Peace.

ISAIAH 9:6 NCV

Prince of Peace, you are the longing of every beating heart. Your love that knows no limits is the dream of all heartsick souls looking for meaning. Every conflict will find its end; wars will cease. But your love will never run out. Your kindness, like a flowing river, will never run dry. Though oceans rise and nations fall, you remain steadfast and secure. You don't experience power shortages; you operate in abundance. I bind myself to you and trust that your unfailing love will carry me through every season and circumstance.

You are better than anything I could ever find, buy, or achieve on this earth, and I won't be satisfied until I'm resting in you. Today, I pause to reflect on your great compassion that reaches out beyond the heavens into my little corner of the world. Spirit of God, I make room for you to come and move in power. Come and mend the broken parts of my life with your healing power.

What area can you invite the Prince of Peace into today?

Vulnerable

"Today in the town of David
a Savior has been born to you;
he is the Messiah, the Lord."

LUKE 2:11 NIV

Emmanuel, your very name states the beautiful mystery of love come down to earth: God with us. You are the incarnation of the saving grace of God, Jesus. What a glorious reality that you came, humbled as a baby, born the way each of us is. In vulnerability, you subjected yourself to the limits of humanity, all while showing us the true heart of the Father. You did not do anything without setting the example of how we can live.

In your living, you poured out love and dignified the dregs of society. In your dying, you united us under the mercy of your sacrifice. In your resurrection, you set the tone for the freedom of your people, that not even death could hold us down. Thank you that as you were with us then in flesh and blood, you are with us now in spirit and truth.

Why is the birth of Jesus significant to remember?

Power Infused

I have saved these most important truths for last: Be supernaturally infused with strength through your life-union with the Lord Jesus. Stand victorious with the force of his explosive power flowing in and through you.

EPHESIANS 6:10 TPT

Lord over all, you are full of every good thing I could ever need. You are the life-source; all strength and power comes from you. If I were to build my strength by training and diet, my own capacity would grow; there is no doubt. However, if I were to give my life to only that, my strength would fail me in the end. Your supernatural strength fills me up from the inside out. It is through connection with you that I find there is an open pathway for everything I need in this life: all the grace, love, patience, compassion, and mercy I could ever want.

What a privilege to receive the bounty of your goodness just by knowing you. Thank you that everything I need is found in relationship with you. What could I want outside of that? You are the power that flows in and out of me; may confidence increase as I grow closer to you.

Are you confident of God's power to change lives?

Fruitful and Fulfilled

Be careful how you walk,
not as unwise men but as wise,
making the most of your time,
because the days are evil.

EPHESIANS 5:15–16 NASB

God of my days, all the wisdom that I'm looking for is found in you. You know how consciously I look for advice so I may live a good and fulfilling life. Laying everything else down in this moment, I come to you, asking for your higher wisdom to flood my heart and mind. As I look into your Word, I see that your ways are different than the world's customs. Don't let me be fooled by empty rules that seem to bring order but really bring uniformity without unity.

Submitting myself to you, I don't need to fear the wasting of my days. May the fruit of my life reflect the fruit of your Spirit. May the product of my time reveal the character of your life in mine. Whether I am running a corporation or playing with a child, if I am doing it with love, the fruit will testify to this. Let me be filled with your revelation today that sets my hope on your higher way.

How are you using your time?

Perfect Father

> "Can a woman forget the baby she nurses? Can she feel
> no kindness for the child to which she gave birth? Even
> if she could forget her children, I will not forget you."
>
> ISAIAH 49:15 NCV

Good Father, that title only lightly touches on the pure goodness of who you are to your children. The kindness with which you see me runs deeper than the roots of the wild fig tree. In the strength of your love, I find my place at your table. As a child of the King, my inheritance is secure. I run to you with my skinned knees; I reveal my deepest heartaches, knowing that you have what I need to comfort me and give me perspective. Where my mom and dad fell short in meeting my needs, you fill in and make up for with your perfect parenting.

Thank you that we never grow out of needing parental guidance, advocacy, and wisdom. You are the one I have continually come back to, and I won't stop now. You are where I find my true identity. Why would I look somewhere else for something that is absolutely and securely found in relationship to you? Perfect Father, I come today just as I am, knowing that I am fully accepted by you.

Do you believe that God loves you completely,
just as you are in this moment?

Increased Humility

Humble yourselves under the mighty power of God,
and at the right time he will lift you up in honor.

1 PETER 5:6 NLT

Holy One, as I look to you, I see my own limitations
so clearly. I cannot begin to fathom the depths of the
sacrifice that you made by sending Jesus, clothed in
flesh and humanity, as a living example of your holy love
made manifest. How could I begin to express gratitude
for something I can barely make sense of? I can't help
but be humbled when I think about your enormous love
for mankind. I have no interest in self-promotion when I
consider the greatness of who you are. As I live my life
connected to yours, I trust that you will be my advocate. It
doesn't matter what I do as long as I do it for you first.

Let my words and my actions align with your kingdom
values. Let my life be like a fragrant offering to you and
a living reflection of your heart. I submit myself to you,
trusting your power to do what no person can. You are
good.

*What can you submit to God that you have been
striving for others to see?*

I Praise You

"You have pain now; but I will see you again,
and your hearts will rejoice,
and no one will take your joy from you."

JOHN 16:22 NRSV

God of my past, present, and future, you hold me together when everything seems to be falling apart around me. You release your love into the gaping wounds that threaten to take me out. Healer, let your salve of grace cover every sore spot, muting the sting that incessantly draws attention to itself. I long to know you in my pain as well as my joy. I know that you meet me in the reality of my circumstances, but you don't leave me there to wallow. You never leave me the same; you are always calling me up, while empowering me with your strength.

I praise you today for your gentle presence that imparts strength and courage to my soul. No one can take away what you give, my good Father, and I open my heart to receive from you today. Here I am; fill your vessel.

What circumstance can you turn into praise today?

Journey Together

The LORD will fulfill his purpose for me;
your steadfast love, O LORD, endures forever.
Do not forsake the work of your hands.

PSALM 138:8 ESV

God of fulfillment, your love guides me through all my days. I will not give up on the work you have started in me, and I know that you won't either. It is the joy of my life to follow you, knowing that you have my best interest at heart in every season. I cannot express the gratitude that fills my soul when I think about how faithful you have been to me. I know that together with you, I can face any obstacle that comes my way with grace.

When I come to the foot of a mountain, I will not be afraid of the climb; your wisdom guides me through. Other times, you move what does not belong in my path, or you move me around it. I will press on with you, knowing I have everything I need precisely when I need it. Here's to the journey with you, Lord. Faithful and steadfast, I walk with you in purpose, looking forward to your grace that meets me wherever I am.

When you look at the journey of your life so far, where do you see God's hand moving you?